LURE FISHING

Also by the Author

LURE FISHING

by A. C. Becker, Jr.

SOUTH BRUNSWICK AND NEW YORK: A. S. BARNES AND COMPANY

LONDON: THOMAS YOSELOFF LTD

© 1970 by A. S. Barnes and Co., Inc.
Library of Congress Catalogue Card Number: 73-88250

A. S. Barnes and Co., Inc.
Cranbury, New Jersey 08512

Thomas Yoseloff Ltd
108 New Bond Street
London W1Y OQX, England

SBN: 498 07429 3
Printed in the United States of America

DEDICATION

To my wife June
and our children—
Carl, Stancie Lee, Christine Ann, and Laura June

CONTENTS

INTRODUCTION

For Angling may be said to be so like the Mathematics that it can never be fully learned; at least not so fully but that there will still be more new experiments left for the trial of other men that succeed us.
—IZAAK WALTON

If man and fish could communicate and pass to each other their thoughts, likes and dislikes, a book on fishing would be an easy task. It would boil down to a textbook of formulas and theorems that could be proved in every instance. Unfortunately men and fish can't communicate.

Consequently a book on fishing must be based on available known facts plus personal experiences, ideas, and theories—theories which unfortunately don't always prove out every time. To further complicate matters, the experiences, ideas, and theories vary from fisherman to fisherman. The ones deemed correct are those subscribed to by the majority. If four of five fishermen agree that red and yellow are the most effective lure colors for attracting fish, then the red and yellow theory is presumed to be correct. Yet there will be times when the lone dissenter knocks the majority's theory for a loop.

This book on lure fishing is based on available known facts and personal experiences, ideas, and theories I have encountered in over three decades of fishing. Yet it could not have been written without valuable help from other fishermen and people in the lure manufacturing business. Acknowledgments must go to Ed Henckel, Jodie Grigg, Cotton Cordell, Doug English, Bob Booth, Dick Kotis, and Nick Creme for the time they spent in discussing lure fishing and in letters answering numerous questions raised by the author.

Acknowledgments, too, are in order to the many outdoor writers with whom I have fished. For years I have picked their brains for ideas and information on lure fishing. On actual fishing trips and in bent-elbow bull sessions such writers as Ken Foree, Henry Stowers, Harv Boughton, Ed Holder, John Thompson, Roy Swann, Grits Gresham, George Kellam, Mike Cook, Curtis Carpenter, Stan Slaton, John Clift, Vern Sanford, Dick McCune, Al Eason, Homer Circle, and L. A. Wilke contributed immensely to lure fishing in general. I picked their brains, and in turn I suppose they picked from my gray matter what little I have learned about lure fishing. We did not always agree, and at times we shot holes in each other's pet theories. But we had a lot of fun doing it.

Special acknowledgment is due Bertha Gill, proof reader and makeup girl at The Galveston *Daily News,* for her sketches illustrating points in several chapters in this book. She did a masterful job of turning my football X's and O's and wavey line diagrams into meaningful sketches.

A. C. Becker, Jr.

Galveston, Texas

October, 1968

LURE FISHING

1

"THE BAIT FALLACIOUS...."

SOME 200 years before the Christian era, the Greek poet Theocritus wrote, " . . . the bait fallacious suspended from the rod." This is a rather stilted way of saying artificial lure, but it is one of the earliest recorded mentions of an artificial lure used in fishing.

Theocritus is credited as being the creator of pastoral poetry. He is thought of as an original poet, and as the "inventor of bucolic poetry," he deserves the reputation. But he also had the reputation of having no scruples about borrowing either from predecessors or contemporaries. So for all we know, the line " . . . the bait fallacious suspended from the rod" may have been borrowed by dear old Theo. Maybe it was even scribed centuries before his time.

Archaeologists have unearthed artifacts that have positively been identified as objects used to catch fish. These artifact lures were made of bone, shell, and other curved-surfaced materials. The curved surface made them spin or wobble when pulled through the water. In modern day fishing we would call it spoon action.

Capt. James Cook, in his writings on world exploration, reported more exactly on the use of lures to catch fish. In visits to the Sandwich Islands (1771-1778) he noted that the natives fished with spoon-type lures fashioned out of sea shells.

Introduction of the spoon-type lure on a commercial basis in the United States is credited to Julio T. Buel. Born near Lake Bomoseen, Vermont, the story goes that Buel as a youngster saw trout rise and strike at pebbles and bits of wood he tossed into the water. He got the idea of soldering a bright strip of tin to a hook and fishing with the contraption. It proved successful. At the age of eighteen he was fishing on a lake one day and took time out for noon lunch. He happened to drop a tablespoon over the side of the boat. It flashed and wobbled as it sank in the clear water, and he noted a large fish rush at it. Some accounts state the fish just rushed at the spoon; others state the fish swallowed it.

13

Anyway it gave him an idea. Young Buel then raided the family silverware. He cut the handles off spoons, attached a hook to one end, and went fishing—quite successfully. Although he considered himself a furrier by trade, he went into the manufacture of spoon lures in 1848. Letterheads of the J. T. Buel Co., which manufactures the Buel type of lures, carry the statement "Established in 1848." This fixes the year of the first commercially produced spoon-type lure in the United States.

History records British anglers as using plug-type lures prior to 1800. They were constructed of fabric and wire and were called Devon and Phantom artificial minnows.

Just prior to 1900 commercial production of plug-type lures was introduced in the United States. It is not certain which came first— the Tango Rush plug or the Dowagiac plug. The applications for patents on these lures were filed in the U. S. Patent Office within a few hours of each other.

James Heddon is generally credited with having been one of the first to commercially produce plugs. The story of how he arrived at making plugs parallels that of Buel and the spoon. Heddon lived on Dowagiac Creek in Michigan. One day while he was waiting for a friend on the banks of the creek, he tossed a bit of wood he had just whittled into the creek. A big bass struck at it and knocked it into the air. The light flashed on in Heddon's mind and that night he whittled several more models at home. He added the metal caps from bottles on each, added hooks, and the next day went fishing. Like Buel with his spoon, Heddon with his plug had marked success. The plug was strictly a surface one.

All this took place in 1896, but it was two years later before Heddon had his plug out on the commercial market. The barn behind his home was his initial factory. The business grew and when 1902 rolled around, Heddon found himself in a new plant built strictly for the manufacture of fishing plugs. Many anglers referred to the early Heddon plugs as "Dowagiacs." Today Heddon lures are known the world over. Obviously they are successful fish-getters. Otherwise how could a business remain in operation so long?

Although records on the development of spoons and plugs are unclear beyond the relatively recent start of commercial production, the history of those lures known as "flies" can be traced back 18 centuries.

An entire book could be written on flies. In fact, a number of excellent ones have been produced. It is not my intent here to go

Earliest of artificial lures was the fly. Above are flies, poppers and jigs that can be handled on fly fishing tackle. The jigs can be used with ultra light spinning tackle.

into flies, for this book is on lures other than flies. This brief mention of flies is necessary, however, because it points out that fishing could be man's oldest sport. Actually it probably would be a toss-up between fishing and hunting. Both were practiced by the earliest man, but back in those days neither was a sport. A fellow hunted and fished in order to obtain food for his belly.

I would guess that fishing as a sport came first. I like to imagine that it happened this way:

Goaded by his wife—a once lovely creature he dragged home by the hair—to become a better providor for the squalling kids beating up the walls of the cave, our hero went a-hunting. He bagged his game, but he knew if he returned to the surroundings of the cave too soon, the missus would find new chores for his strong back and weak mind. Well, on the way back he chanced upon a lovely stream shaded by huge trees, so he decided to siesta in the shade. To better while away the time, into that mind his missus called "weak" popped the idea of dangling a line in the water. Whatever he tied on the end to make it easier for tossing out attracted fish. Lo and behold, he had discovered a new pastime —a sport—that beat flagstoning the cave entrance or hewing out a new room. The fish he caught—and took to the missus—served as the crutch upon which he leaned as tangible evidence that his sport was not just a waste of time.

I like to think of fishing as our first sport, and I like to think it happened this way.

There is a parallel to the caveman story in the thinking of to-day's angler.

"We haven't had fish in a long time. Think I'll go up to the lake for the weekend and bring back a mess." These remarks have been heard by wives more often than there is money in the national debt. It is just an excuse—a crutch—to enjoy a fine sport. Fish solely for eating can be obtained quicker and cheaper by a simple visit to the fish market.

2

I FOOLED A FISH

I was about nine or ten years old when I first discovered that fish bite things other than other fish. I was spending a few weeks with a cousin near Anahuac, Texas. His folks' homestead was on the banks of Double Bayou, and my cousin and I spent many hours down on the boat dock floating toy boats. At the time I was particularly proud of my little boat, which I had taken great pains to saw and whittle out of a block of wood. At the stern it had a paddle wheel that was powered by rubber bands. I painted the bottom of the boat red and the top white. My cousin had a similar boat which he had made.

We were having great sport winding up the paddle wheels and then letting the boats run out toward the center of the bayou. We had threads attached to the boats so we could pull them back when the paddle wheels stopped. My boat—that beautiful red and white thing I had created with my own two hands—was nearing the end of its run when a black cigar shaped alligator gar arose from the depths, opened its jaws wide, and promptly crushed my creation to splinters.

I was crushed—mentally—to see my creation, which at the time seemed to represent the whole world to me, broken beyond recognition. I carved out a lot of wooden boats after that, but none seemed so dear as that first one.

It was when I was about 14 or 15 years old that I bought my first artificial lure—a red and white sinking plug. Gad, how I fished that lure that summer in the surf at Galveston, Texas. I fished it for hours on end, day after day—and caught nothing. It seems I had bought a lure that had no instruction sheet packed in the cardboard box. I would just cast the thing out and let it lie on the bottom. I had just about reached the point of feeling that stories of fish being caught on lures were all lies. I made up my mind to reel in the lure, cut it off and throw it away. In my anger at having spent 50 cents I could 'have used for something else, I did not just reel in the lure. I reeled furiously and repeatedly jerked the rod tip to hurry the "useless chunk of wood" ashore.

Then it happened. Something hit with a jolt. I did not have a reel with a drag device and as line stripped off, it burned the skin raw on my thumb. I finally stopped the run and got the plug back to shore by walking backwards up the beach. The rear treble hook on the lure was firmly imbedded in the mouth of a redfish. I never did weigh the fish, and I will have to guess that it weighed about six or seven pounds.

When my father came home from work that afternoon, I greeted him on the front porch with fish in one hand and the plug in the other.

"Look! I fooled a fish! I caught a fish on my plug!"

My exclamations were loud enough to be heard all over the neighborhood.

In the weeks that followed, I visited the library and read everything I could find on artificial lures. I even worked up the courage to ask a couple of grouchy fishermen for advice. They turned out to be grouchy only until they learned that I had a true desire to become skilled at lure fishing. Then they became the most helpful souls in this world, and today I can't even recall their names. I wish I could, for they certainly deserve a place in this book.

Although this book is about lure fishing, this does not mean that I fish lures exclusively. I still frequently fish with natural baits. But when I am fishing alone or with skilled lure anglers, I use hardware only. Whenever I take a newcomer fishing with me, I invariably take along natural baits. There are two reasons for this, and they are important because they eventually dovetail into the lure fishing picture.

A number of fishing trip invitations extended me come from people who feel that since I am an outdoor writer, I should know all the answers. This is far, far from true. I learn something new, odd, or strange about fish on every trip, and I have been doing outdoor writing for 22 years. The day when I stop learning about fish will be the day I drop dead, and I hope that day is many, many years off.

If the time is available I accept every fishing invitation. I know full well that the person inviting me is out to pick up from me all the information he or she can. Well, they don't have a monopoly by any long shot because I am picking their brains right back for new ideas, theories, and stories—stories either for my newspaper or for magazines. No, I don't mind a fishing companion picking my brains at all. In fact, some of the hardest pickers have supplied me with the meat for magazine articles that brought in rather healthy checks.

But back to the reason for lugging along natural bait. This is a sure-fire guarantee of catching fish, maybe not the species you specifically seek, but nevertheless fish. I am very much interested in my companions catching fish. Many of them are only luke-warm fishermen to start off with, but after they get enough successful trips under their belts, they become solid citizens in the fishing fraternity. This is the fraternity that keeps outdoor writers in business. You might view it as my way of advertising for new readers of my writings.

Sooner or later every fisherman feels the urge to graduate from high school bait fishing to college class luring. The sooner he makes the transition the better, for when he becomes an accomplished lure angler, he also becomes a better bait fisherman. His experience with lures teaches him not to just cast out a natural bait and let it rest on the bottom or suspend motionless beneath a float on the surface. Through lure fishing he learns the importance of action . . . and he then starts imparting action into natural bait fishing.

Perhaps the greatest advantage of catching a fish on a lure is psychological. Fish are supposed to hit natural baits, for after all this is the stuff they eat. Catching a fish on a lure represents a personal triumph for the fisherman, proof that he really is smarter than a fish. He may not shout it out loud as I did, but consciously he triumphs over the thought "I fooled a fish."

There is a sequel to the little boat I lost to an alligator gar, and perhaps it can be looked upon as poetic justice.

Some 25 years or so after the boat tragedy, I was back on that same Double Bayou hunting squirrels. It was during the hot part of the day that I decided to just loaf on the boat landing, and to have something to pass the time more quickly I dug my rod and reel out of the car trunk. I tied on a large red and white floating plug and started casting it. In the true sense I was not fishing. I was just playing with the lure to see what kinds of action I could get out of it. I had been doing this for about 15 minutes when a large black shape eased up near the surface. It eyed the lure suspiciously and I put everything I had into it to make the lure appear to be something injured and in trouble.

Finally the gar decided to take it. I struck at the right time to bed the hooks in the fish's tough mouth. With the help of my .22— every time the fish surfaced I whammed a slug into it—I landed the gar. When the fish was eventually dragged out on the bank, I guess-estimated the weight at 50 pounds.

Somehow I feel that the red and white plug had exacted revenge for the little red and white boat that some 25 years earlier had been destroyed by a fish. Although it certainly was not the same alligator gar, the poetic justice is there in that the same species of fish that had destroyed was in turn destroyed.

And, again, I had fooled a fish.

3

LURE PRESENTATION

LURE presentation is all important. If it is done crudely, don't expect much success. Good lure presentation calls for precision casting, line control, and skillful rod and reel manipulation. These are things a fisherman can only learn with practice and which cannot be accomplished overnight. Those "fishing nuts" one so often sees casting a practice plug on the front lawn are not just passing the time, nor are they nuts. They are practicing to sharpen their casting accuracy. They practice to see how close they can drop the plug alongside a tree trunk or how well they can drop the plug in a hole in the hedge.

This accuracy counts when it comes to actually fishing a lure. Most skilled anglers agree that accuracy is far more important than getting extreme distance. As far as I am concerned the only time distance really counts is in the surf where it is important to get the lure as far out to sea as possible.

Lure presentation varies considerably from fresh to salt water, and to do the job intelligently one must know something of fish habits and characteristics.

Let's take fresh water fish first. Keep in mind that almost all fresh water fish are non-migratory in nature and rather slow swimmers. This means a slower and more deliberate style of lure fishing is required than in salt water. Most fresh water fish tend to hang around underwater obstructions. Consequently it is important to know something of the river or lake bottom topography—the location of boulders, sunken logs, flooded timber stands, brush piles, etc. These are the places where most fresh water fish spend much of their time.

Fresh water lure fishing is a lot like filling out your income tax return. Don't do it haphazardly. Instead check and re-check.

Let me use a personal example, going back to a time when I

When waters are glassy slick, surface lures can be very effective. These lures attract fish by sound and disturbing surface of water. They are most effective in coves and relatively shallow water.

only had two or three years of fresh water fishing experience under my belt. I was fishing in a central Texas lake and had eased up to a spot where a huge log fingered out into the water. The end of the log and a brush pile angling back from it formed a small triangle of open water near the shoreline. I was using a top water chugger since it was at a time of the year when the black bass were hitting well on surface lures.

Fishing flooded timber stands calls for accurate casting and ability to work lures around tree trunks and floating lily pads.

I worked from one end of that log to the other and must have made a half dozen casts without so much as even a water swirl from a fish. I contemplated casting over the log and into the open triangle of water. A reluctance to risk snagging the log and possibly losing the lure caused me to resist the urge. This is a common fear of most beginning lure fishermen. They hate to lose lures. This is a mistake. Frankly if you can't stand losing lures every now and then, the thing to do is to forget about them and stick strictly with natural bait fishing.

As I mulled over the situation, another angler eased his boat around the point. He paddled up nearby and asked me what luck I was having. "I've fished this place hard," I replied, "and I haven't raised a thing." Had I chanced upon him and gotten the same answer to the question, I would have moved to a new spot. But he did not. He made several casts alongside the log as I had done and raised nothing. Then he deftly plunked the lure into the open triangle of water. I was interested in seeing how he would get the lure over the log without snagging up.

He chugged his plug several times and then when it was just

a few feet from the log, there was a mighty splash and the lure vanished in a cloud of spray. A few minutes later he landed a fat three pound bass, although he had to paddle up to the log to keep the fish from becoming tangled in underwater brush. Before moving to a new area a little later on, the fellow picked up a smaller bass from the same pocket. Before he got it, however, he twice had to paddle over to the log to free a snagged lure.

At the time, I had the skill to plunk my lure in the triangle, but I lacked the courage to face up to the fact that occasionally one has to risk losing lures to snags.

In fresh water fishing, never make one or two casts to a spot and then move on. Thoroughly work every foot of the water within casting range. Experiment with retrieves and fish at different depths. You might even switch lures occasionally, but I must warn that this lure switching bit can become a disease. Changing lures

Waters like this are ideal for artificial lure fishing, particularly surface plugs and floating-diving plugs. Lures must be worked close to the tree trunks where fish usually hide. (Courtesy Louisiana Tourist Development Commission)

every few minutes seriously cuts down one's fishing time.

Presentation in fresh water fishing is of utmost importance when the water is glass slick. Remember when the lure strikes the water it has a startling effect on the fish. If you are using a floater or floating-diving plug, allow the plug to lie at rest on the surface at least long enough for all the surface ripples to vanish. Give the fish time to overcome the initial fright. Then work the lure gently, and with frequent pauses. I know one old East Texas codger who actually takes five minutes to fish out a cast when using a surface plug, but I am not going to knock his style because he catches a lot of fish. I don't fish quite that slow. I fish out a cast in about two or three minutes.

This long wait before retrieve will not work with sinking plugs. If you do wait, the odds are great that the plug will sink down into the bottom brush and snag up. The retrieve on the sinking plug must be started within a few seconds after it hits the water. If you start the retrieve immediately, the plug will run at a depth of about a foot below the surface. Plugs sink at a speed of about a foot a second. Consequently a five second wait means the lure will work about five feet deep. It is important that you know the depth of the water so that you won't allow the plug to sink into the bottom brush. Sinking into the bottom brush is okay if your plug is equipped with weedless hooks. If the water is deep, you can work a lure at various depths on a single cast simply by pausing for a few seconds during the course of a retrieve.

Remember how long each pause was. This is important when you get a strike. One day the fish might be 10 feet down, and the next day only five feet down. A lure worked too far above or below the fish will get little action. Also in this connection remember whether the fish hit the lure on a slow or fast retrieve. Every time you get a strike or catch a fish, be sure to "copy-cat" on succeeding casts the action you put in on the successful retrieve. I don't believe in knocking success.

The spoon is fished in fresh water in much the same manner as the sinking plug. But a spoon sinks much faster than a plug and a five second wait will result in the spoon plummeting to a depth of about 15 feet instead of five. Slow and fast retrieves can be used with spoons. If the spoon is equipped with weedless hooks, it is okay to let it sink to the bottom and down into the brush. You may lose a spoon once in a while when the weed guard flips open, but this is just one of the hazards of the game.

Spoons, diving plugs, jigs, and spinners are good choices for fishing rivers with rapids such as this on the Taltson River in the Canadian Northwest Territories.

Lead-head jigs and jig-worms must be worked along the bottom and in a slow crawling or hippity-hop manner. These lures come with weed guard attachments and because of the design of these lures they are less apt to snag than either spoons or plugs.

Now to lure presentation in salt water fishing. Here you will find much faster swimming fish. Salt water fish hang around underwater obstructions but rarely in the motionless manner of most fresh water fish. The salt water cousins seem to be always on the move.

Again proper lure presentation calls for working the lure at various depths and speeds, but there is a different demand for accuracy in casting. This is because of the speed of salt water fish and the fact that they are constantly on the move.

In shallow water the fisherman should work his lure around points of land fingering out into the bays, around reefs, through flooded grass flats, in and alongside of shallow troughs and cuts.

Since the water is shallow, the angler frequently will see swirls or "vees" in the water. These are caused by moving fish. The fisherman must be on the alert to note the direction in which the fish appear to be moving. Never cast right on top of the swirl or "V" because by the time the lure strikes the water, the fish that caused the surface disturbance may be 10 to 15 feet beyond the point.

Cast well ahead of the path in which you suspect the fish are moving. Then work the lure across that path. If the lure passes in front of the fish's nose at the right time, you can expect a wedding. It is a lot like the crossing shot in duck hunting, where you shoot not at where the duck is but at a point where the duck will arrive on a collision course with the column of shot. This is the proper way to fish sinking plugs and spoons in shallow salt water.

When it comes to deep water, it is a matter of casting all around the boat, experimenting with speed of retrieve and lure action. When you get a strike or fish, "copy-cat" the successful retrieve.

In fresh water lure fishing, if an area does not produce after you have given it a thorough workout, the accepted—and approved—practice is to try a new location. In the space of a day you may work 30 or 40 different spots. Frequent moves, however, are not necessary in salt water fishing. Salt water gamefish are constantly on the move, and with the sea being as open as it is, it is foolhardy to attempt to follow the schools. The one exception is in offshore fishing where you can see the schools of surface feeders and you are in a boat fast enough to keep up with school movements. For general lure fishing in inshore waters, stick with a known fish-producing area. When one school leaves, another is likely to move in. This may happen within minutes, while at other times it might require a wait of an hour or so.

The most successful lures in salt water are those that work below the surface. Strict floaters will get salt water fish at times, but not to the degree of consistency found in fresh water fishing. I am convinced after 30 years of fishing that floaters in salt water work best at night or during the passage of rain showers over shallow water areas. Either way they must be lures that make a lot of surface commotion and act like crippled baitfish.

This heavy rain bit, incidentally, has great appeal in fresh water fishing. Splashing rain that disturbs the surface seems to have a tremendous attraction in getting gamefish to work right up to the surface, where they start feeding with reckless abandon.

Lead-head jigs and jig-worms are deadly in salt water fishing,

This is a slow-flowing river. Surface and floating-diving plugs can be used along the rocks on the left side of the river. Spoons and deep running plugs are more effective for the deeper water in the center of the river.

but the manner of presentation is entirely different than that used in fresh water. The lead-head jig in particular is fished at a fast, steady retrieve or a fast hippity-hop along the bottom. The exception to this comes in the winter when low temperatures cause the fish to become sluggish. Then a slow hippity-hop is necessary.

Best lure fishing in a river with off-color water is near the banks. Flashy spoons and rapidly vibrating underwater plugs get the best results.

The jig-worm that has been popular for years in fresh water found its place in salt water only in recent years. I think this was mainly because of a reluctance of anglers to change over to something new that looked totally foreign as far as salt water baits were concerned. It took me three years to convince one lure manufacturer to make jig-worms expressly for salt water fishing. Today he is making good money off his product.

The jig-worm is excellent for speckled trout, striped bass, and redfish. These worms are considerably shorter in length than models used in fresh water. They are also deadly on Spanish mackerel,

king mackerel, and dolphin. The only trouble is these sharp-tooth
fish rip them to shreds in a hurry. A jig-worm is good for about
three fish before it is reduced solely to the lead-head. The manner
to work the jig-worm for fish in the mackerel family is to cast and
use a fast retrieve in order to keep the lure near the surface or to
troll.

The floating-diving plug has its place in salt water fishing, but
mainly in casting for offshore migratory surface feeders. I have
used these lures with great success offshore, but I recall only rare
occasions when these lures were hit while floating at rest on the
surface. The strikes always came when the lure was being retrieved and riding a few feet beneath the surface. I have taken
offshore fish on sinking plugs but only when the retrieve was started
soon enough to keep the lure riding just a few feet below the surface. I have had very little success with sinking lures worked down
deep in offshore waters.

One lure manufacturer, Doug English of Corpus Christi, Texas,
feels that lure vibration or wiggle is more important in fresh water
than salt water. This is what he says:

"There is so much noise in salt water that I don't think that
the vibrations can be picked up by a fish at any appreciable distance. Salt water is not at all like the quiet lake or still pond. Our
experience has shown that lures with a slow, wide-sweeping wiggle are better fish producers in salt water than are the fast wigglers."

Quite frequently in clear water—and especially so in fresh
water—the angler can see the fish he is seeking. If the fisherman
happens to be wearing polaroid glasses, his ability to see underwater objects is increased considerably.

Lure presentation to a fish that can be seen calls for plunking
the hardware into the water beyond and in front of the fish. Then
it is worked back in such a manner as to cross the fish's line of
travel. Casting in front of the fish is no problem but casting beyond
the distance the fish appears to be is another matter.

If you cast to a spot a couple of feet beyond where the fish
appears to be, you are in good shape. If your cast happens to be
a little short and the lure appears to land right on top of the fish,
don't get excited. You did not hit the fish. To understand this consider the properties of matter and light. Matter or substances that
permit the passage of light "bend" the light rays. This is known as
refraction.

A flashlight beam directed at the wall strikes the wall at the

Even though this east Texas bayou is choked with water plants, it can still be fished with lures by poling boat right through the plants and fishing jigs and plastic worms wherever openings appear.

point of aim. A flashlight beam aimed at the wall but passed first through a pane of glass set at an angle will strike the wall a bit off of where you aimed. If a tank of water is substituted for the pane of glass, the beam will strike the wall at still another spot. The "bend" or refraction will be noticeably greater when the beam is passed through the tank of water than the pane of glass.

This same thing happens when you look at a fish underwater. It is never where it appears to be. Actually it is closer, and how much closer depends upon how far the fish is below the surface.

Consequently the cast that appears to drop the lure on top of the fish's head is actually a few feet beyond the fish. It is the cast that drops the lure a few feet short of where the fish appears to be that gets one into trouble. This is the lure that so to speak "hits the fish on the head." A lure dropped that close will invariably spook the fish, unless it is feeding voraciously or is in a truculent and fighting mood.

Remember, what happens when you look at a fish in the water also happens with the fish when it looks at you. He sees you at a spot other than where you actually are. This is one difference. When you looked at the fish, it appeared farther away than it actually was. The fish, however, sees you closer than you actually are.

The sketch at the end of this chapter illustrates how man and fish see each other. The solid lines indicate the location of man and fish, while the broken lines indicate where each appears to the other.

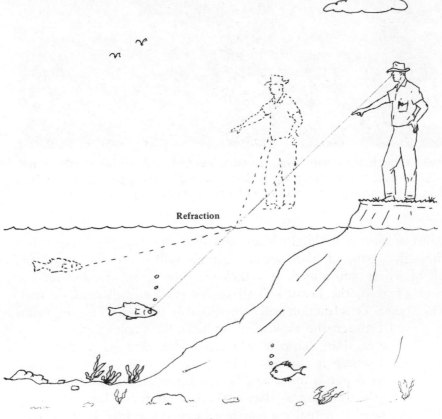

Refraction

4

APPEAL TO MOODS

IF you suppose that fish strike lures out of hunger, you are right—but only partially right. Actually hunger is only one of several reasons. One day it might be the predominant reason, while the next day it may be for an entirely different reason. The fisherman has no way of knowing the reasons for strikes from one day to another. Consequently in order to be successful with hardware tackle, he must be inquisitive and open minded enough to do a lot of experimenting.

Every fellow who tosses a lure seeks first to present the lure in an enticing manner that will cause the fish to develop an appetite for food. If he is fishing an artificial shrimp, he will attempt to make the lure act like a real live shrimp. This means working it slow and bouncing it along the bottom, where shrimp are normally found. On the other hand an artificial minnow would be fished nearer the surface. The normal retrieve for such a lure in salt water would be rather fast, with occasional twitching of the rod tip to give it darting motion. The object is to make the lure act like a frantic minnow.

The speed of the retrieve for a given lure will vary from fish to fish as well as from salt water to fresh water. Let's take a simple lead-head jig as an example. This lure will take both fresh water and salt water fish, but the manner of working it varies considerably. In fresh water this lure is usually fished slowly. Even when trolled behind a boat, the speed of the troll is slow. The same lure used in salt water must be retrieved considerably faster, although there are a few species of salt water fish that can be taken by slowly bumping it along the bottom.

Why the difference?

A study of fish bodies—particularly the tails—will provide the answer.

Fresh water fish are adapted for small bodies of water. Not

only that they are non-migratory. Consequently most of these fish are not built for distance traveling or for speed. Note how many species are deep-bodied—and closer to being oval in shape rather than elongated. Their tails are more fan-shaped than forked. These fish are slow moving. Consequently a very fast retrieve or troll can actually take the lure away from these fish.

Almost all species of salt water fish are much more streamlined. For one thing many are migratory in nature and in the span of a year will travel several thousand miles. Because of this their bodies are shaped for travel and speed. Their tails are deep-forked, hard-spined, and quite strong. As a result the jig trolled for these fish must be done at a faster speed than for most fresh water fish. Trolling in a fresh water lake is best at a speed of one to three miles per hour. In salt water the same lure would be trolled for Spanish mackerel in a speed range of three to six or seven miles per hour. If king mackerel are involved, the speed would be closer to 10 miles per hour, and in the case of a few species like bonita and some members of the tuna family the trolling speed may be even faster.

This faster speed is necessary in salt water in order to keep up with the school of fish—or more correctly to stay ahead of the school. Spanish mackerel will hit a jig trolled at a speed of one mile per hour, but you won't catch many because the school will soon pass the boat. It is the other way around with the fast troll in fresh water. In this case the fast troll ends up with you running away from the fish.

Most all species of fish can swim fast for a short distance, but only those with streamlined bodies and deep-forked tails are able to maintain speed over any considerable distance. In a way speed can be considered a mood. People are like that, too. Some like jet travel; others prefer to go by auto.

A fish's body takes on the temperature of the water, and as a result fish act in different manners according to the temperature. Except for species adapted for cold water, fish become rather dormant when the water temperature drops. This is especially true with salt water fish of what can be called the resident species. Migratory salt water fish are constantly on the move for waters of suitable temperature and head for the tropics in the winter.

For example, consider the styles of lure fishing for speckled trout in Gulf Coast waters where there is a considerable temperature difference from summer to winter. In the spring and fall when water temperatures are reasonably mild, specks will hit artificials worked at a fast retrieve. These fish get rather loggy during the dog days of summer and work best to a slower and more erratic retrieve. In the winter these fish will be in deep water and the only way you can get them to hit consistently is to work the lure dead slow on the bottom.

This same holds true with fresh water bass. Relatively fast retrieves will work in the spring and fall, but slow retrieves are necessary during the heat of summer and cold of mid-winter.

Water clarity plays a part in retrieve speed. The rapid retrieve used in gin clear water will lure nix in off-color water. The reason is quite obvious—the fish must be able to locate and see the lure before they can strike it. All wobbling lures set up vibrations in the water, and these vibrations are sensed through the lateral lines on a fish's body. Thus the fish can use sound waves to home in on a lure. The only trouble with a fast retrieve in off-color water is that you usually have the lure reeled back to the rod tip before the fish has time to locate it.

Consequently the hardware angler fishing off-color water should use a slower retrieve. An erratic retrieve of fast reeling for a few feet and then a pause of a few seconds is most effective. The fast reeling sets up sound waves the fish can pick up. The pause gives the fish time to move within vision range of the lure. This vibrate-pause, vibrate-pause retrieve is quite deadly in that it is an excellent imitation of a crippled minnow.

Now if the crippled minnow retrieve is so deadly in off-color water, then why not use it always in clear water too? The main reason is that too long a pause will give the fish too much time to eye the hardware and perhaps recognize it as something phony. This is especially true in fresh water fishing. An exception to the case in fresh water is the black bass. I have had bass follow but refuse to hit moving lures. I have also had them rise stealthly under a motionless floating plug, eye it for what seemed like hours and then suddenly strike with a mighty splash.

Some fisherman—including some successful lure anglers—fail to fish their lures all the way in. They fish the lure properly until it is about 15 feet from them. Then they retrieve it with lightning-like swiftness in order to make another cast. This is a mistake. Fish the lure all the way back to the rod tip, for you never know if there is a fish lurking down deep out of sight. You may not see the fish, but the fish can see the lure. Just about the time the fish decides to make a pass at the lure, you jerk it away with a lightning retrieve.

I have caught many bass and northern pike in fresh water and speckled trout in salt water within 10 to 15 feet of the boat. In some cases I could even see the fish following the lure. It is my guess that the fish only had half-hearted interest in the lure, but when they saw the shadow of the boat, they figured it as a safety haven for that strange thing swimming in front of them. Rather then let the "thing" escape to safety, the fish make their pass. I believe their mood was one of letting nothing go unchallenged.

The proper way to fish out that final 15 feet or so is to dip the rod tip close to the water and slow down the retrieve. Once I had a two pound bass nail my lure when it was only several feet from the rod tip. The incident sticks in my memory because that was the only fish I caught in four hours fishing that particular day.

All lures have instruction sheets packed in the box or instructions printed on the back of the box. Study these instructions and make it the first rule of the day to follow them. Give the lure a fair test following the advice of the manufacturer, but don't be hardheaded about it. If following instructions fails to produce fish, then show your own initiative—and experiment. Often a sort of "off-beat" style will produce remarkable results.

The only way I can explain this is to point out that fish—like people—have moods. They may be sluggish and indolent one day but frisky the next. They may be hungry for long periods, but then there are times when they feed only slightly and irregularly. They are creatures of habit but totally unlike people when it comes to eating. As a result of custom and habit, humans usually eat three time a day—about 7 A.M., at noon and again around 6 P.M. Fish are not so punctual about their feeding, consequently the fisherman is often out seeking them at a time when they could care less about food.

This means that if a fellow is to have any success, he will have to make an appeal to the fish on some grounds other than hunger. These appeals must be made to arouse curiosity, anger, or territorial protection.

This is where speed of retrieve comes into play. The slow retrieve is essentially one aimed at arousing a feeding instinct. Fish are quite a bit like people in that they are lazy about some things. When they are hungry, they find it far easier to catch a crippled minnow or shrimp than to chase a frisky one. But if the fish has a full belly, it will most likely ignore the crippled critter. There are a few exceptions. For example, take the bluefish, a fine salt water gamefish. These fish will slash through schools of baitfish and kill for kill sake only. They will feed on the fish they kill, regurgitate the meal, and go on another killing spree.

But let's get back to fish that behave in a more normal fashion, for these are the ones you will meet up with most often.

After giving the slow retrieve a fair trial, start your experimenting—fast retrieves, fast reeling, and pauses, etc. Think in terms of making the fish either curious or angry. It is a little like that one fly in the kitchen. It flitters around and really does not bother you much. You shoo it off a few times with a wave of your hand. But after a while—even though it may be on the other side of the kitchen—its buzzing starts to grate on your nerves. So you stir from your laziness and teach it a lesson with finality with a fly swatter. It is the same thing with something that pesters a fish.

The most vivid experience I had along this line was with a black bass lying along side a log in the shallow end of an East Texas lake. Since I was wearing Polaroid glasses, I could see the fish quite plainly. I must have made a half dozen casts to that fish with a floating-diving plug. I worked the lure tantilizingly slow by the fish and all it did was to turn around and stare. Since the slow retrieve obviously was not going to get results, I started making fast retrieves so that the lure wiggled vigorously as it flashed by the fish. This got only stares on the first two casts. The third retrieve seemed to make the fish restless for it swam a little closer to the lure, perhaps for a better look see.

On the fourth cast the fish moved back alongside the log, but it swam up and down its length like a stock broker who had just seen the Dow-Jones averages dive. On the fifth cast, the fish charged out and appeared to try to chase away the annoyance with a swipe of its tail. On the sixth cast, Mr. Bass took the flyswatter attitude, charged right in and grabbed the lure with a vicious strike. The fish, of course, ended up in the boat. I was curious to learn why the fish had acted as it did. So I gutted it and examined the stomach contents. It contained a half dozen minnows, two small frogs, and something else I could not identify because it had been broken down by digestive juices. Quite obviously that fish had a full belly, and it did not strike my lure because of hunger. It was simply a case of me being able to make the fish angry.

There are times when black bass will strike anything that drops near them, regardless of the type of retrieve used. This is during the spawning season when they protectively guard their nests.

Jodie Grigg of Whopper-Stopper has some views on this and states the following: "Fish definitely strike lures out of hunger, curiosity and anger but with hunger heading the list. I think surprise should also be included. How many times have you had a fish strike immediately after the lure hits the water? Maybe you would not call it surprise but more of a reflex action, possibly a defensive action. I am not sure, but it is food for thought."

I believe fish have another mood, too. I feel it is one of playfulness, and the only way I can support this belief is to cite examples. One involved the use of live bait and the other lures.

I was bay fishing for speckled trout. The water was about five feet deep and I was using live shrimp for bait. I had a float on my line so that the shrimp suspended about two feet off the bottom. Time after time I had the float bob vigorously but not go down. Each time I reeled in I found the shrimp still on the hook. Sometimes the shrimp would be dead; other times it would still be alive. I decided to examine the bait carefully after each cast. After I had checked four shrimp I decided on a course of action. Each of the shrimp showed tooth marks on its body in addition to having a few of its feet nibbled off.

Obviously the fish hitting were not hungry but were merely playing with the bait much like a cat plays with a spool. My style of fishing had been one of casting out and gently flicking the rod tip to give the live shrimp extra action. So I decided to change the style. As soon as the bait hit the water, I started a steady retrieve. The first few casts produced nothing. Then wham-o—a strike. And I reeled in a fat speckled trout. After that I caught a lot of fish and frequently had three or four specks follow the hooked fish right up to the boat. The change in fishing style had transformed the playfulness of the fish from a game of touch football to one of tackle, with the usual serious consequences. I believe in the idea of fish playing and frolicking because what happened on that trip has happened many more times in my fishing career.

Now to the case with the lure, which like the live shrimp case has happened often.

Again I was fishing for speckled trout but this time in considerably deeper water. I was using a Plugging Shorty plastic shrimp and hippity-hopping it along the bottom. This method had

produced a lot of fish in the past. But on this particular day I was
getting nothing, although I distinctly felt the lure being bumped
repeatedly. I finally figured out what was happening after I hooked
what I thought was a monster of a fish. Man, how it pulled! When
I boated it, the fish turned out to be a speck slightly less than two
pounds in size. Yet it pulled like a ten-pounder, the reason being
that the rear hook on the lure had snagged into the fish's side. I
guessed that all those bumps I had previously felt were fish playfully pumping the lure with their bodies or swatting it with their
tails.

So I went to a fast retrieve, and immediately got results. It
stirred the fish to the point where they started hitting the lure with
their mouths. Every trout I caught that day was taken on the rear
hook, an indication that the fish really were not feeding but only
playfully nipping at the lure. Proof that the fish were not hungry
was evident when I gutted them and found each chocked with
food.

The drawing at the end of this chapter illustrates differences
in body shapes and empenages in fast and slow swimming fish.
Those with squarish, soft-rayed tails are slow swimmers and non-
migratory. Fast swimming, migratory fish have deep-forked tails
with hard spines. Migratory and fast swimming fish have elongated
bodies, while the slow swimmers have deep oval bodies with dorsal
fins running from neck to near base of tail. These fins are soft-rayed.

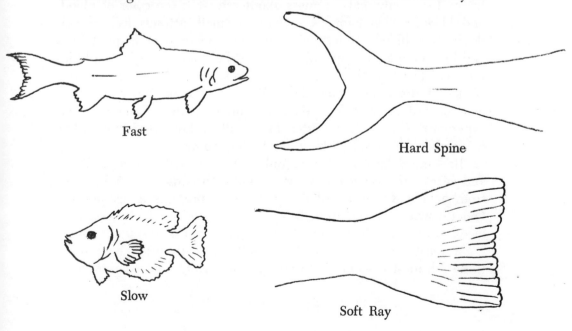

Fast

Hard Spine

Slow

Soft Ray

5

RED ON YELLOW

WHEN it comes to the deadly poisonous coral snake, there is a little verse that goes like this:

> Red on black,
> venom lack;
> Red on yellow,
> kills a fellow.

You might ask what snakes have to do with lures and fishing. Really nothing except as a point of illustration on the subject of color. The poisonous coral snake has the same colorful bands found on another snake that is totally harmless. These bands are red, yellow and black. On the harmless snake the black bands separate the yellow from the red, but on the deadly coral snake the red and yellow bands touch.

You will find every color imaginable on lures, but there are two colors that are most attractive—and deadly—for fish. These are red and yellow. Just exactly why they are so attractive, I don't know. I can only make a guess about red. It is the color of blood, and blood, which happens to have a smell, attracts fish. If you doubt that blood attracts, just cut your finger over a quiet pool and let a couple of drops fall on the surface. Then watch the blue-gills and perch slash around in the slick. As far as yellow is concerned, I don't have any clear-cut ideas, except perhaps that it may be visible from long distances under water. From personal experience I have had better luck with yellow than any other color when it comes to fishing in off-color water.

Red and yellow are not the only colors attractive to fish. White and black are also good. White possibly because it can be seen from a long distance under water. Black presents a distinct silhouette when viewed from below and is deadly effective on surface lures when fished at night or on dark overcast days.

A great many experiments carried out with black bass show these fish most susceptible to red, yellow, white, and combinations of these colors. Another quite effective color for bass—especially when it comes to deep-running and bottom-bumping lures—is purple and its shades into violet.

Exhaustive tests with fish have turned up that green and blue are the least effective colors, even though many of the baitfish that gamefish feed upon are various shades of green or blue. It is my personal belief that in the case of lures these colors that it is lure action and skillful manipulation on the part of the angler that really gets the fish.

Let me cite a few personal experiments with lure colors. A number of them involved trolling jigs for Spanish mackerel and king mackerel. In order to make the tests fair, identical jigs were used but of different colors. The jigs were trolled four at a time—all at the same speed, distance, and depth behind the boat. The red and yellow jigs outcaught the blue and green jigs 10 to one over an average of 12 tests made during the space of a month. Water conditions varied from gin clear to off-color and from slick to rough. Yellow produced best results in off-color and rough water. Red ranked slightly ahead of yellow in gin clear water. Green and blue produced absolutely nothing in off-color water.

I conducted similar tests in fresh water for black bass. In this case the lures were plastic worms and they were fished on the bottom. Tests were made on 15 separate occasions. The colors used included natural worm, yellow, red, black, green and purple. All the tests were made in water approximately 20 feet deep. The most fish and strikes came on lures in the following order: purple, red, black, yellow, green and natural. A similar set of tests were later made in shallow water, three to five feet deep. In these tests red was far out front and then in order came natural, purple, black, green and yellow.

From all the tests I have made I rather suspect that yellow is the best color when the lure is moved rapidly through the water. In the case of the plastic worms, all the fishing was done at a slow crawl.

There is no question that fish can distinguish colors, although the colors may not appear to be as true as they do to the human eye. Perhaps they just appear in shades of gray. If man could ever establish positive understandable communication with fish, he might be able to learn to fish the seas dry. Until that time comes, all we can do is go on theories, suppositions and educated guesses. When

Note differences in lure appearances when light source is from opposite directions. In the top photos with the viewer between light source and lures, the markings on the frog and the minnow are clearly visible. In the lower photos the lures are between the viewer and light source, which is the way fish usually see surface lures. Frog and minnow appear mainly as silhouettes, although transparent body of minnow permits body stripes to register.

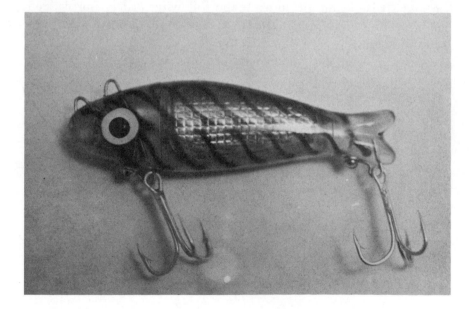

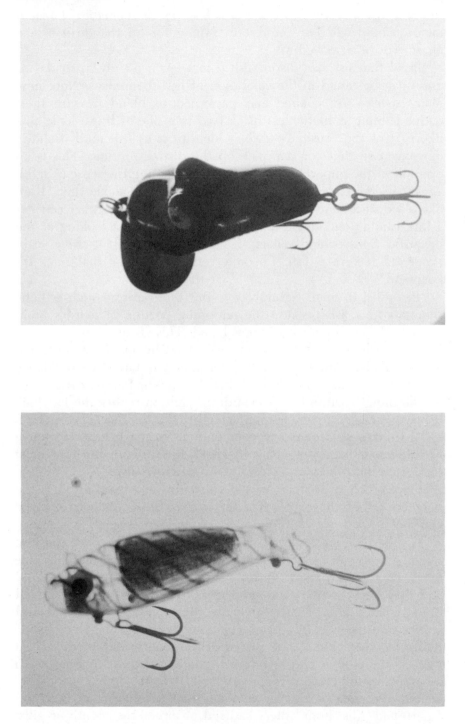

catching fish becomes as exact a science as mathematics, I fear a lot of people will lose interest in fishing for all the thrill of the chase will be removed.

Proof that fish can distinguish colors—even if only in shades of gray—can be found in the coloration of fish themselves. Note how many species are colored and patterned to blend in with their native habitat. A motionless black bass in a pile of brush looks just like part of the brush. You won't identify it as fish until it shows movement so that you can pick up the distinct outline. This is an example of the importance of motion in attracting the sense of sight.

Whenever I walk up to the lure display in a tackle shop, I am like a kid in a candy store. Everything looks wonderful. I can get a lure catalog and spend an enjoyable evening just looking at the beautiful finishes and colors. I find myself thinking time after time: "If I were a fish, I would certainly go for that one. It's beautiful."

Beautiful to man, certainly yes. But there are no such esthetic thoughts in a fish because the reasoning portion of a fish's brain is infinitely small and poorly developed. This "beauty" bit captures far more fishermen than fish. There is good in this, however, for if a fellow feels a lure is attractive for fish, he will have the confidence to fish the lure as it should be fished. He might feel he caught fish on the thing because it was beautiful, while in reality the fish took it because either action or sound caught its attention.

If it takes 101 colors and combinations to make lures attractive to fishermen, I am not going to knock it. After all the lure must first catch the fisherman before it can catch the fish.

Confidence is just part of the game. In fact, mentally it is the biggest part of the game. If a fellow has the confidence that he can fool a fish with a lure, he will accomplish his goal.

A fisherman may swear by a "green shad" finish. Since the lure manufacturer must catch the fisherman first, the maker will come out with a "green shad" finish. These lure makers are not stupid and they know that if their product is to sell and continue to sell it must catch fish. They also know the effectiveness of red and yellow in attracting fish. They come out with a true "green shad" finish, but they add a slash of red at the mouth and another slash to indicate gills. I checked "green shad" finishes put out by 25 different manufacturers, some nationally known, others sectionally known. Eighteen of the "green shad" had red slashes at both the mouth and gills. Four others had red at either the mouth or gills.

Plastic shrimp at top is molded in solid color. Model at bottom has several colors molded in and will present more lifelike appearance in water.

Only three had no red whatsoever, and it was interesting to note that none were nationally known lures.

At this writing I have before me the color chart of a successful plug manufacturing company. The chart lists 53 patterns or finishes. Thirty-nine have red some place in the pattern and 22 have yellow. Only eight have neither red nor yellow in their finishes. Granted all the reds noted were not "five engine." They ranged from pink to deep red.

The chart of another manufacturer—this one a sectional company—lists 39 color combinations and finishes. Red is some place in the finish on 36 patterns. Yellow figures in on 31. Only three finishes are completely without red or yellow. One is all blue, another all green, and the third is solid black.

On all the charts checked, even those lures predominantly blue or green had either built-in flash (silver beneath the surface) or enough white on the sides to indicate scales. There is that flash to aid in the attraction of sight.

The views of some of the lure makers are interesting. For example Jodie Grigg, general manager of Whopper Stopper, Inc., reported:

"Color preference varies with the time of the year. Overall sales lean toward natural finishes such as perch, shad, frogs, etc., with predominately yellow and red and white combinations running right along with the natural finishes."

Most of the lures put out by Grigg's company are designed for fresh water fishing.

Cotton Cordell of the Cordell Fishing Tackle Co., of Hot Springs, Arkansas, had this answer to questions about the most effective colors:

"In our tests in salt water we find that metalized lures in silver, blue, gold, pearl yellow and pearl white are real good. For fresh water fishing shad colors are best with perch colors running second, but not close."

As to the importance of color on a lure, Cordell had this to report:

"If the lure doesn't have proper action, the real good color is nil. A good action plug, however, can be effective in any color at times."

Grigg added the following about lure colors:

"My experience has been that yellow patterns and black have been good in early spring. In late spring, summer and fall all patterns produce at one time or another. In winter months, solid white and nickle plated lures have been good to me. Mainly, however, I think water conditions and the food supply govern pattern selections more than anything.

"To illustrate both points, two of us were fishing Lake Texoma on a partly cloudy day in early spring. We caught eight bass from four to six and a half pounds in a two hundred yard stretch on a yellow Hellbender making three passes over the course. In the interest of experimenting, we switched patterns several times and could arouse no interest on anything but the yellow.

"On my first trip to Canyon Lake near San Antonio, I asked my fishing partner, who regularly fished the lake, what the bass normally fed on. His reply was a heavy stock of perch and a few shad. My selection was a green perch Hellbender and 12 of 14 bass averaging a little over four pounds each was the result. This also included pattern changes with no results except the two caught on a black and white ribs Hellbender.

"I could site several instances when a certain lure has produced well, but I don't think we could prove much. I think consistently catching fish is all in finding them, choosing a lure and color that is appealing at the same time and one that can be worked or fished at the depth the fish are found."

6

SIGHT AND SOUND

THE brain—whether it is human, animal or fish—is divided into many sections and the development of the different sections varies. That portion of man's brain devoted to reasoning is rather large. The reasoning section of a fish's brain is a very small percentage of the entire brain. Except for a few species of fish, the optic portion is the largest part of their brain. This means that a fish's actions and reactions are geared basically to sight. This in turn means that if a lure is to arouse the interest of a fish it must appeal to its sight.

A fish's sight can be captured by two means—recognition of a familiar food object or motion. This is the reason so many lures are made as replicas of marine objects upon which fish normally feed. Thus we can assume that if the lure looks enough like the real thing and good enough to eat, then fish are likely to strike it. This explains why a motionless lure resting on the surface of the water is often hit by a fish. The lure's silhouette resembles something upon which the fish feed.

But it often takes more than the mere recognition to gain the sense of sight. Motion and sound rank next as sources for the attraction of sight. If you are walking down the street and hear a strange noise, you immediately turn your head toward the source of the sound. Then your eyes come into play to pinpoint and recognize the cause of the sound. This same thing happens with fish in connection with lures that produce sounds. The sound catches their attention, motion pinpoints the location, and then if the lure looks enticing enough they do something about it. At times it may be only a closer investigation of the lure. Other times it will be an outright charge and strike. The reaction depends upon the disposition of the fish and the moods of hunger, curiosity, anger, or fear. The first three moods—hunger, curiosity, and anger—can lead to the fish investigating or striking the lure. Fear will cause it to retreat and vacate the premises.

Concave shape of face on this Heddon Lucky 13 plug will cause lure to make "chug" sound when rod tip is popped. On steady retrieve the face will cause lure to wiggle slowly just a few inches below the surface. At rest this lure floats.

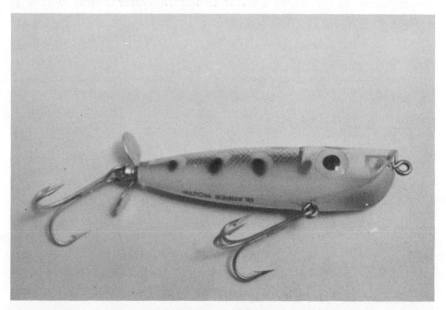

This Blabber Mouth plug makes a "plip-plip-plip" sound on retrieve due to the whirling propeller blades. Shape of face will cause lure to attempt to "climb out" of water. With skillful rod manipulation, angler can make this lure "jump" out of water and over snags.

Fear is the one mood you do not want to arouse. All living creatures with brain power possess fear, for fear is the one mood that insures immediate survival. Fear can be caused in the fish by haphazard lure presentation, like dropping it too close to the fish or right on top of the fish's head. It can also be caused by the angler making sudden or foreign noises.

Motion or movement will attract the attention of sight. This is the reason a speaker in a crowded auditorium will always ask persons asking questions to either rise or hold up their hands. Sound can give the speaker the location of the questioner in a general sense as being in the front of the gathering, the rear or off to one side. But he needs some sort of motion or movement to single out the specific individual.

Translate this into fishing. If there is a school of minnows working near the surface, the ones that move about the most are the ones that capture your attention, as well as the attention of any gamefish that may be nearby.

A fish can hear sound through its inner ear. In addition a fish also has the ability to feel sound—or vibrations—through a special development in its body. This is called the lateral line, which is

Inverted airplane-like wing lip on this Jitterbug plug produces a steady "gurgle" sound when lure is retrieved. Plug floats at rest.

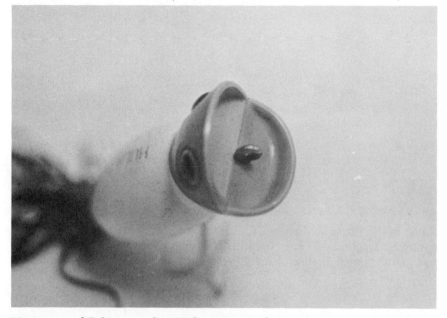

"Open-mouth" face on this Hula Popper plug makes it an effective surface noise-maker. Depending upon force applied in twitching rod tip, this plug will make a "chug" or a distinct "pop" sound.

actually a series of pits and tiny openings in the skin and scales of the fish. Behind these pits and within the body of the fish there are nerves in a sort of tube. A tiny branch of this nerve extends under the openings of the pits in the scales. Vibrations, even slight ones, can be felt through this lateral line and cause a reaction in the fish.

This lateral line is quite pronounced on some species and barely discernable on others. The general belief is that the lateral line serves as some kind of sonar that enables fish to detect and locate objects without having to see them. Quite likely this lateral line acts as a sort of defense mechanism to warn fish of impending danger.

Since the nerves in the lateral line are exposed almost raw at the surface, the fish is able to pick up the slightest of vibrations. The lateral line is quite pronounced on the black bass and extremely sensitive to touch. Try this experiment with the next black you catch. Hold the fish by grasping it by the lower lip. This immobilizes the fish to the point where it holds its body practically rigid. Now take a soda straw and direct a gentle stream of air ALONG the lateral line. The fish will react immediately by quivering. Gentle

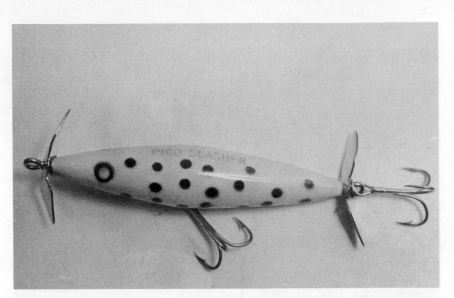

Front and back propellers on this Pico Slasher surface plug revolve in opposite directions. This is helpful in keeping lure body from spinning and putting twist in line. Lure's propellers produce a rapid "plip-plip-plip" sound.

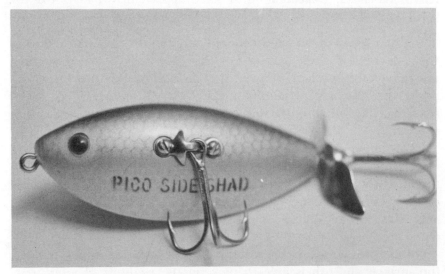

This Pico Side Shad is a surface lure that combines sound (propellers) with erratic motion. Lure lies on its side in water and when rod tip is twitched sharply, lure will dart to one side or the other and dive a few inches. Action is much like that of a dying minnow.

streams of air directed against the fish's back, belly, head or fins will produce no reaction from the fish. Now take your finger and gently stroke the fish's back, belly or head. Again no response. Using the same gentle touch, run your finger any place along the lateral line and the fish will try to shake free.

Don't believe this talk about the "silent sea." It is anything but that. Water—five times denser than air—is an excellent conductor of sound, and small sounds that might be lost in the air are magnified in the water. Recordings made underwater present a bedlam of sounds. No, the sea is not silent.

The lure industry's first capitalization of sound was in the strictly surface plugs. The sounds produced were a "chug," "plop," or "gurgle." The "chug" and "plop" sounds were made by constructing plugs with concave faces. The "gurgle" was made by adding an inverted metal lip to the front of the lure. When the lure was pulled through the water, the lip made the plug attempt to climb out of the water rather than dive. Another surface sound was that of a "sputter" created by adding a propeller to the lure. Models are available with props front or back as well as at both ends. All of these sounds are produced by breaking or disturbing the surface of the water, and as a result they are readily heard by the angler.

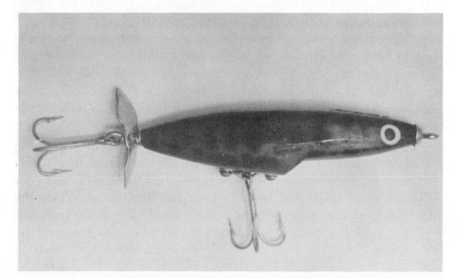

The "step" on the bottom of this Shadrac plug enables angler to make it jump out of water. It can be fished effectively in brush-filled waters.

Underwater sounds—or vibrations—are produced by wiggling plugs, wobbling spoons, spinners, and propellers. The more rapid the wiggle or wobble, the more pronounced the vibrations.

The lure company public relations boys grabbed this rapid wiggle bit and made the most of it in the mid-1950s. They hailed underwater sound as an attraction for fish as the greatest thing since radar, and there was a wild race involving a number of lure companies to see who could come up with the most vigorously vibrating lure. They developed some real dandies—lures that vibrated so fast that the pulsating throbs could be felt right up the line to the rod tip. You knew your lure was wiggling right if your rod tip quivered like the rhinestone in an Egyptian belly dancer's navel. It was not all palaver by the PR boys either, for those rapidly vibrating lures proved most effective as fish-getters.

These lures proved double barrel attractions for fish. There was the sound—or vibrations—to attract attention, and then there was that fast wiggle—or motion—to catch sight attention.

These rapid wigglers—or vibrating lures—are superior when it comes to fishing in off-color water. I have fished them with marked success in both salt and fresh water where the sub-surface visibility was reduced to about three feet. Almost all lures can be made to wiggle rapidly if the retrieve is fast enough. The advantage of the lures built specifically to produce violent wiggles is that the action can be obtained with a normal—and even slow—retrieve. This is most important in off-color water where the fish must be given time to locate the lure. A fast retrieve in turbid water often results in the lure being reeled back to the boat before the fish ever gets a chance to move in closer enough for visual contract. The slow retrieve possible with those lures designed to wiggle rapidly means the lure is in the water for a longer period of time on each cast.

Currently some makers are using additional means of adding sound to their lures. Some put a few small shotgun pellets inside the hollow plastic bodies. I have one lure that has a propeller mounted on a shaft that runs through the lure body. When the propeller revolves, a ratchet on a shaft inside the body puts out a steady "tick-tick-tick." Personally I don't think this lure will be very successful. First, a considerable force of water is needed to overcome friction in getting the ratchet to work. This means a very fast retrieve and consequently the lure won't be in the water very long. When trolled behind a boat, the ratchet's "tick-tick-tick" is drowned out by the boat engine and propeller noises. The only

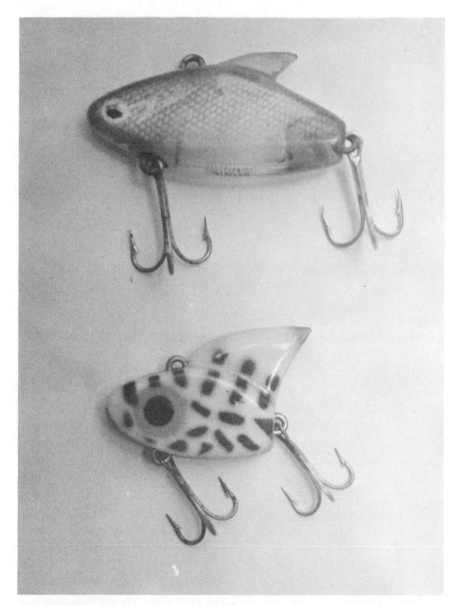

The Heddon Sonic (top) and Sailfin (bottom) are examples of lures that produce sounds underwater. These lures vibrate extremely fast when retrieved. The pulsation of the vibrations can be felt all the way up through the rod.

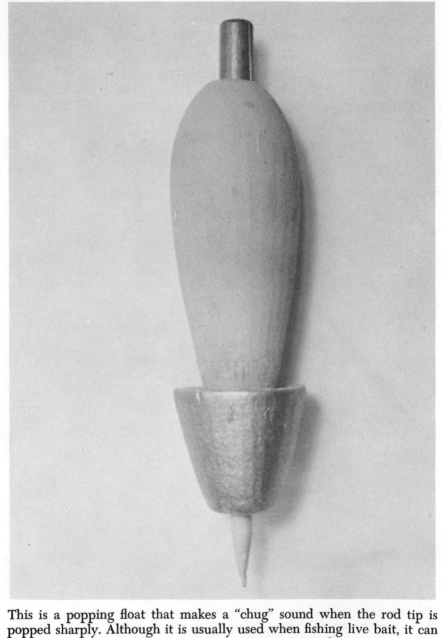

This is a popping float that makes a "chug" sound when the rod tip is popped sharply. Although it is usually used when fishing live bait, it can also be used in lure fishing as a teaser. Lure is rigged to suspend three to four feet beneath the float. Jigs and sinking plugs can be used effectively under this float. The rig is ideal for keeping sinking lures just above bottom brush.

hope I can see for this lure is in using it in a river with a swift current. A further disadvantage of this lure is that the metal shaft and metal sleeves in which it rides tend to corrode badly, especially in salt water.

Speaking of boat propeller noises, I might point out that in salt water trolling noise-maker lures are not really necessary. Boat props seem to have some sort of special attraction for salt water migratory surface feeders. A great many boats ranging from ocean-going freighters to commercial workboats, fishing boats, etc., daily ply our waters. The people on these boats all have one thing in common, the dumping of their refuse and trash over the stern. Perhaps these fish associate prop noises with easy feeding.

I have done some flying in light planes out over the Gulf of Mexico and over areas where boats trolled for king mackerel. When the water was calm, I could easily see these schools of kings from the air. It was most interesting to note how often they changed courses to home in behind the trolling boats. They would make every turn and circle made by the boats.

7

ONE FOR ALL

THE three musketeers may have been "all for one and one for all," but don't expect to find any such thing in artificial lures. Any time you walk into a tackle store and a salesman tries to sell you a lure that will serve for all kinds of fishing, view that character with suspicion. He is either a con man out to take your money or completely ignorant when it comes to fishing.

Lures will catch all kinds of fish. The lure developed for fresh water fishing will take salt water fish and vica versa. But there is no single lure that will produce satisfactorily for all types of fishing. The all-purpose lure is just a myth.

Lures can be categorized as floaters, floater-divers, deep runners, and bottom-bumpers. You can jury rig a floater to make it run deep underwater, but when you do so, be fully prepared to accept the fact that it will lose some of its action and effectiveness. All lures are designed for a specific purpose, and any radical change in presentation will serve only to defeat the purpose.

Take the spoon as an example. It is designed to wobble and dart beneath the surface. How far below the surface it works depends on how long the angler waits to start his retrieve after each cast. The spoon also can be bumped and jigged on the bottom. It can be worked on the surface by starting the retrieve just as it hits the water and continuing to reel extremely fast. A spoon is about as close as one can come to an all-purpose lure. It can be fished surface, sub-surface, or on the bottom, but there are limitations. The primary purpose of the spoon is to wiggle and wobble through the water like a baitfish. This is accomplished when it is fished sub-surface with a steady retrieve. When you jig it on the bottom, you lose a lot of that wiggle and wobble. Then when you skitter it across the surface, you lose all the wiggle and wobble. A spoon is effective as a fish-getter only when it is in motion. It does no good whatsoever lying on the bottom, and since it will not float, you can't cast out and allow it to remain motionless on the surface.

You run into this same sort of thing with plugs and jigs. Each is designed for a specific purpose—and in some cases for certain species of fish. But no single lure—plug, spoon or jig— will serve as a combination floater, floater-diver, deep-runner, and bottom-bumper. Over the years a few "all-purpose" lures have been put on the market, but it is interesting to note that the life of each was quite short.

I can recall years ago when lures were strictly categorized for fresh water or salt water. Prior to World War II days no self-respecting salt water fisherman would think of using a fresh water lure in the brine, nor would a fresh water angler take a salt water model to the lake. This situation still exists but in far less degree than back in the pre-WW II days. Consequently we have some lures that can be considered all purpose to the degree that they are effective fish-getters in both salt water and fresh water.

Some of these lures were designed for both salt and fresh water fishing. Others got reputations as universal producers strictly by accident—or rather due to the inquisitiveness of some lure anglers.

Let me cite some personal experiences as well as experiences encountered by some of the lure manufacturers themselves.

Right after World War II a small group of outdoors writers spent three days fishing Galveston, Texas, offshore waters. The Fred Arbogast Co., of Akron, Ohio, sent down a packet of lures for each fisherman. At that time the Arbogast Company was putting out lures designed specifically for fresh water fishing. One of the writers, a fellow who considered himself to be an expert on everything, griped so much about a "damned outfit sending fresh water lures for salt water fishing" that I became quite angry since I was one of the hosts for the trip. We were catching king mackerel by trolling feathered jigs. It reached the point where I took off my feathered jig and put on a red and white Hawaiian Wiggler, which happened to be an old Arbogast standby for black bass. And wham—wham—wham—I caught kings. Several other fellows on the trip tied on Wigglers and had good results, too. The Wigglers did not prove to be more effective than the feathered jigs, but they did prove to be fish-getters in salt water.

Then there was the case of the plastic worm that proved to be so deadly on black bass in fresh water. It is now a highly successful lure for speckled trout, redfish, stripers and flounders in salt water. Yet this worm was specifically designed for fresh water bass fishing.

Years ago Doug English of the Doug English Bait Co., in Corpus Christi, Texas, put out the Plugging Shorty, a rigid plastic shrimp lure. It was designed for salt water fishing, especially for speckled trout and redfish on the Gulf Coast. It did and continues to do a tremendous job. Then somebody found out it was a good fish-taker in fresh water. English has told me that at certain times of the year the Plugging Shorty sells better on the lakes than on the Gulf Coast.

Consider the Cordell Hot Spot put out by Cotton Cordell of the Cordell Fishing Tackle Co., of Hot Springs, Arkansas.

Cordell wrote me the following about this bait: "The Hot Spot was made to catch bass in Arkansas. It has also proven to be a fish-taker for other kinds of fish. It was proven on kingfish (king mackerel) with 117 caught in three hours. Coho salmon, salt water stripers and rockfish in North Carolina have also been caught in number on the lure."

The points brought out in this chapter don't mean you should go out and stock up on just any makes or types of lures. Even though salt water and fresh water models can be "flipflopped" so to speak, the best practice for lure stocking is to buy those designed specifically for the kind of fishing you do most.

But at the same time don't expect to find that "all for one and one for all" lure. It has not been made yet, and I doubt that it ever will. I fear that the many aspects of fishing plus the combinations of weather and water conditions mixed in with the moods of fish would be enough to turn the stomach of an electronic computer. Figuring your income tax is child's play in comparison with lure fishing. This comparison is not made to alarm you and frighten you away from fishing, but rather is a challenge and one that should make you feel elated when you "fool a fish."

8

FISHING THE PLUGS

PLUGS can be divided into four categories—surface, floating-diving, deep diving, and sinking. No one plug can be made to perform all four tasks, although with the use of sinkers a lure can be made to perform two jobs. But remember use of the sinker will limit the plug's action to some extent.

Let's consider the accepted methods of fishing plugs in each of the four categories.

SURFACE PLUGS

These are typical surface lures with propellers, lips or faces designed to make noise and create disturbances in the water when retrieve is made. They are most effective when fished in calm, clear water.

These are plugs that float on the water and remain on the surface through the entire retrieve. They are fished much slower than plugs in the other three categories. The surface plug is the one with which an expert lure angler may spend as much as five minutes to fish out a single cast.

Floating plugs are designed to get at fish in shallow water and as a result are used most frequently near the shoreline. This is also the plug that calls for extremely accurate casting since the angler will be shooting for little pockets, holes in the lily pads, and around logs and stumps.

The accepted method of fishing floaters is to cast out and allow the lure to remain motionless on the surface. Then twitch the rod tip lightly, and then let the plug remain motionless again. Do this several times. Then reel the plug in slowly for a few feet and repeat the process all over again. When the water is calm, use a light or soft twitch of the rod. If the water is rough, then a more vigorous rod pop is necessary because the noise of the plug's surface "chug," "plop," or "sputter" must be heard over the lapping wavelets. Keep in mind that all surface plugs are in the noise-maker class.

Surface lures are seldom used in deep water unless there is evidence of fish schooling right at the surface. Even under this condition, the surface plug is a rather poor choice. The number one choice for this situation is the floating-diving plug.

FLOATING-DIVING PLUGS

The floating-diving plug is primarily a shallow water lure, although it can be used effectively in deep water when fish school on the surface.

This plug at rest floats on the surface. Its lip or the shape of its face will cause it to go beneath the surface when retrieved. With a steady retrieve, the floating-diving plug will work 12 to 18 inches below the surface. Its wiggle is rather slow, even when retrieved rapidly.

Floating-diving plugs are excellent for shoreline fishing or in water where bottom weeds are heavy. The accepted method of fishing is to cast out and allow the bait to remain motionless for a few seconds. Then start a slow retrieve which will cause the plug to go beneath the surface. An occasional jerk with the rod tip will cause the plug to dart and speed up its action. This darting action is much like that of an injured minnow.

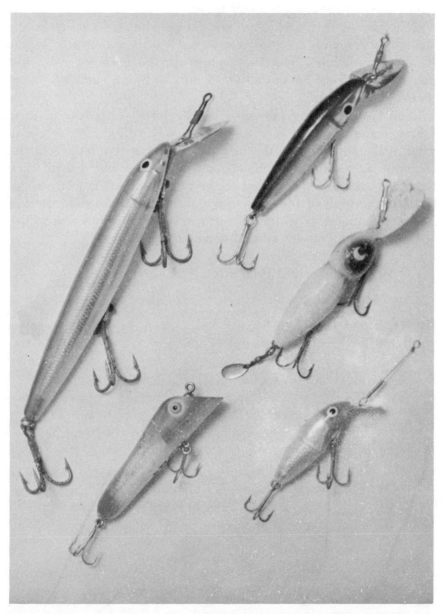

These are typical floater-diver plugs. At rest these plugs float. On retrieve they dive. Speed of retrieve will govern how deep they dive.

It takes time to fish out each cast properly. In addition to the steady retrieve, frequent pauses can be made allowing the plug to climb back to the surface each time.

The floating-diving plug is a fine choice when it comes to fishing shallow water with a lot of submerged weeds and brush. In the hands of a skillful angler these plugs can be made to swim just above and over the cover and are deadly in luring gamefish out of their hiding places.

The floating-diving plug is a deadly lure for dawn and dusk fishing under certain water conditions. When the water is glassy calm, make your cast so the lure plunks just a few feet from the shoreline. Let it rest motionless for a bit. Then start a dead slow but steady retrieve. The speed of the retrieve must be just enough to cause the front of the plug to wiggle underwater while the tail creates a tantalizing "V" on the surface. If the plug has a propeller at the rear end, you get an additional "sputter" noise.

DEEP DIVING PLUGS

Most deep running plugs such as these are weighted and come without diving lips. They sink rapidly. Long-bodied plugs have slow wide-sweeping wiggle. Short-bodied plugs have rapid vibrating wiggle.

The deep diving plug is one that barely floats when at rest. There are also some models that normally sink. Usually these lures have long lips that will cause them to plane down sharply. Their wiggle varies with the speed of the retrieve.

These plugs are designed specifically for fishing dropoffs, deep channels, cuts, and holes. Whether the model floats or sinks, it will dive rapidly when retrieved and can be made to work at various depths. The retrieve on fishing this lure must be started with a pop of the rod tip and rapid reeling in order to get the lure quickly to the desired depth. Then the retrieve is slowed down so that the plug can be kept at that depth. These plugs have a particularly tantalizing action near the boat for they are retrieved almost straight up. As they are being reeled up, they will sheer off from side to side much as a minnow will do when it sees the shadow of a boat.

In one respect deep diving plugs have a near-weedless feature. The metal lip is long enough so that when it hits bottom or brush,

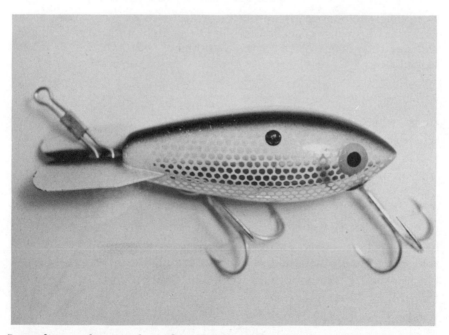

Long lip on this Bomber plug makes it dive steeply to great depth on fast retrieve, making it excellent for fishing deep holes. When retrieve is stopped, plug will wiggle back to surface. When snagged this lure can often be freed by allowing slack line and letting plug "back out" of brush.

Note differences in diving lips on these floater-diver plugs. Lure at left with short lip will run shallow, while one at right with large diving lip will run quite deep. When retrieve is stopped, both lures will float back to surface.

the hooks are far enough back so as not to snag. The deep diving plugs which have buoyancy will float slowly back to the surface when slack line is allowed. You can work this plug right down into the brush, and then by slacking off the line allow it to "back out" free of snagging up.

This type of plug can be used quite effectively in shallow water if the bottom is level and sandy. Here the method of operation is to quickly get the plug to the bottom. Then slow the retrieve and make the lure "walk" along the bottom. The long metal lip will raise little clouds of sand and offer an excellent imitation of a small baitfish rooting the bottom for food. This same plug is also excellent for trolling in deep water.

SINKING PLUGS

Sinking plugs do just what their name implies. They sink. Some sink fast; others sink slow. They come with and without lips. When an angler uses one of these plugs, he must know how fast it sinks.

Usually this plug is allowed to sink to the bottom and then

retrieved in a hippity-hopped fashion, with occasional pauses to allow it to rest motionless on the bottom. If the retrieve is started before it strikes bottom, then the plug will work at the depth at which the retrieve began. Thus it is important to know how fast it sinks. Some of these plugs go down like rocks. Others descend as slowly as a feather in the air.

Sinking plugs can be sub-divided into three classes—shallow, medium, and deep. Those that sink slow are for shallow water down to about five feet in depth. The medium runners can be worked in water up to about 12 feet in depth and sink considerably faster than the shallow water models. The deep sinking plugs are those that go down like rocks. Their speed to the bottom is usually accelerated by a lip. These are worked most effectively by either jigging or hippity-hopping along the bottom.

Surface, floating-diving, and deep diving plugs are made either of wood or hollow plastic. Sinking plugs today are almost always made of solid plastic. Before the introduction of plastic into the lure business, sinking plugs were made of wood with sufficient lead added to make them sink.

Some underwater runners like this Cisco Kid have jointed bodies for extra wide-sweeping wiggle.

The angle of dive on some floating-diving and deep diving plugs can be regulated by gently bending the metal lip. This, however, is not to be attempted unless so advised in the instructions that come with the lure. Lip-bending on some models will seriously alter the plug's action.

If it is necessary to replace hooks on any of these plugs, be sure to do so with sizes identical with those originally attached. A change in hook size can seriously upset the action of floating-diving and surface plugs. It takes a major change in hook size to cause a noticeable change in the action or attitude of deep diving or sinking plugs.

Surface and floating-diving plugs should be used with monofilament leaders. If a wire leader is necessary, it should be flexible and as fine as possible. Even then you can expect the extra weight of the wire to alter the action of the lure to some degree. Wire used for leaders on deep running lures should also be flexible, although it won't alter lure action nearly as much as in the case of top water plugs.

Quite often wind will dictate the type of plug used for casting. There is never any problem casting with the wind, but the shape and design of many plugs make them brutes to cast into a stiff wind. The hardest of all to cast into the wind are the floaters since they are rather large size and relatively lightweight. The fast sinkers are the ones that cast best into the wind. They have weight and are of a compact and streamlined design.

9

FISHING SPOONS

WHEN it comes to artificial lures, more anglers fish spoons than any other kind of hardware, most likely because spoons hold an attraction for all species of fish. Additional reasons for the popularity of spoons: they are easier to cast, especially when it comes to distance casting, and they are easier to work.

The spoon is strictly an underwater lure, although later in this chapter I will explain how they can be fished to some degree on the surface.

Almost all spoons have a wobbling action that can be regulated from slow to rapid depending upon the speed of retrieve. A few spoons will spin and a few streak through the water with absolutely no action, but these are specialty spoons used mainly in trolling. All spoons have one thing in common. They start to sink as soon as they hit the water. The depth at which a spoon works depends upon when the angler starts his retrieve and the type of retrieve used.

The universal retrieve for spoon fishing is steady reeling. The lure will work at the depth when the retrieve is started and remain at that depth all the way in, unless the retrieve style is altered. The steady retrieve is quite effective in salt water where baitfish normally swim rather fast. Extra action can be put into this retrieve by frequently twitching the rod tip to make the spoon dart erratically. This gives it the behavior of a wounded minnow.

There is an even more effective spoon retrieve that is particularly deadly in moderately deep water. For want of a better name it can be called the "dying minnow." The retrieve is started a second or two after the spoon hits the water. Reel in rapidly for a few feet and then pause. Keep this up until the spoon is recovered. Each time the fisherman pauses in the retrieve, the spoon will sink with a fluttering leaf action. When the reeling is started again, it should be done with a sharp twitch of the rod tip. This will make

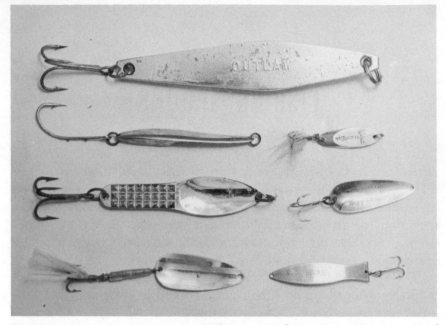

Spoons come in many sizes and shapes. Outlaw spoon at top is used mainly for trolling. Others are light enough to be handled on casting or spinning tackle.

the spoon dart upward a bit, much like a dying minnow will do in attempting to climb to the surface.

Remember when using this retrieve-pause-twitch style, the spoon is worked at a little deeper depth after each pause.

The spoon, too, can be worked right on the bottom. The style here is to allow the spoon to sink all the way to the bottom before starting the retrieve. Then start with a sharp twitch of the rod tip. This will cause the spoon to "jump" off the bottom. Follow this with rapidly reeling for a few feet. Then stop and allow the spoon to sink back to the bottom. Wait a few seconds and then repeat the action over again.

Drift-jigging is another method where spoons pay off. This is effective in very deep water and when one is drifting in a boat. You can either cast out and let the spoon sink the length of the line used in the cast, or you can peel off a definite amount of line and simply drop the spoon overboard and allow it to sink. The style here is to let the boat drift with the current or wind. Dip the rod tip into the water and then sharply lift it as high as possible. This will cause the spoon to dart upward. Then drop the

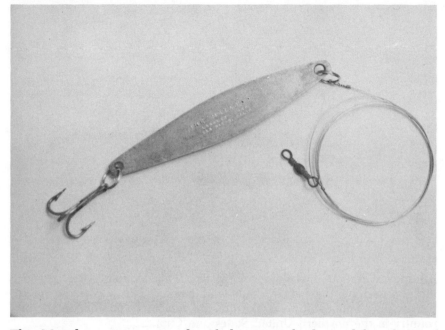

This Matador spoon is rigged with long wire leader and barrel swivel for offshore trolling. Wire leaders will not hamper spoon action on trolled lures if the leader is attached to lure with split ring or snap.

rod tip quickly back into the water and allow the spoon to flutter down again. Pause a few seconds and repeat the operation. Fish strikes usually come when the spoon flutters back down. This is a most effective way to catch lake trout when a school is located in deep water.

Spoons are ideal when it comes to trolling and especially so in salt water and in deep fresh water lakes. The depth at which a spoon is trolled is governed by the amount of line out (more line, deeper running), speed of the boat (slower speed, deeper running), line and trolling sinkers. For deep water trolling anglers should use monel wire line since its weight will often eliminate the use of sinkers, which can become quite bothersome when fighting a fish.

Now to that method of working a spoon right on the surface. Actually it is a form of skittering, except you don't do it by sweeping a long pole back and forth.

The spoon-on-the-surface method is used extensively in the south in shallow salt water bays and it is popularly called "skip-spooning." It is an art that a fellow can learn to master in a matter of a few casts and it is easiest when broad spoons are used.

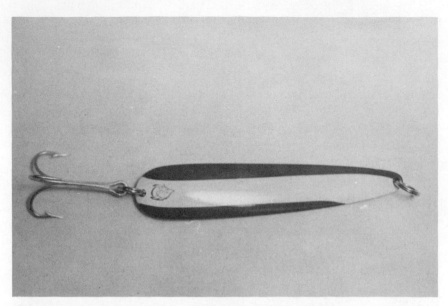

All spoons are not nickel or gold-plated. This Eppinger Sea Devle is nickel-plated on the concave side and painted red and white on the convex side. Spoons finished like this are extremely popular in the lake country in the northern United States and Canada.

Some metal spoons are partially or completely encased in plastic. Top is Cordell Gay Blade and bottom is Bomber Slab Spoon. Compact size and weight of such lures give angler the advantage of long casts.

Make your cast. Reach out as far as you can with your rod, keeping the tip pointed to where the spoon will strike the water. Start reeling rapidly a split second before the spoon hits the water. When the spoon hits the surface, sweep the rod tip up and hold the rod pointing straight upward high over head. The full retrieve is made by reeling rapidly while holding the rod high. If the retrieve is started just before the spoon strikes the water, it is easy to keep it skipping across the surface. The action is quite similar to that of a frightened minnow or mullet.

The skip-spoon retrieve can be combined with an under water retrieve if the angler pauses reeling when the lure is about halfway in. With a long, whippy rod and just the slightest of a pause, a skilled skip-spooner can let his spoon sink briefly and then work it back up across the surface. Skip-spooning is an extremely deadly method of fishing around the edges of flooded salt grass flats. It is most effective when the water is slick calm at night or when the sky is heavy overcast.

A spoon, unless it is very light, is an excellent choice for distance casting, even into the face of a stiff wind.

10

FISHING THE PLASTIC WORM

"IT'S not a plug—it's not a spoon—it's super worm!"

This take-off on the introduction to the old Superman series on television fits to a "T" the plastic worm's reputation in fresh water fishing.

Nick Creme of the Creme Lure Co., of Tyler, Texas, and Akron, Ohio, came up with the plastic worm that has revolutionized bass fishing; and when it comes to digging out the blacks, the Creme worm is one of the best single lures ever devised. These plastic worm lures are the ones that stir bass into action when every other

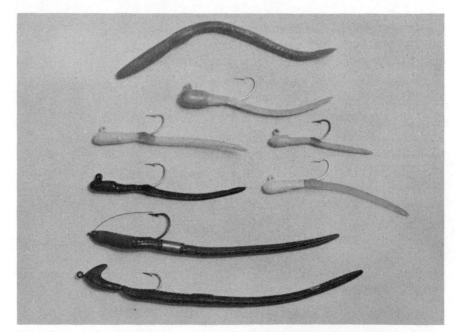

This illustrates a few of the variations of the plastic worm. Most popular rigging is with lead-head jig. Some use the complete worm, while others employ short tail portion. The worms come in all colors of the rainbow.

kind of hardware draws blanks. They are especially deadly when the fish are deep in hot weather.

It certainly cannot be called a plug—nor can it be called a spoon. It is a perfect imitation of a real worm right down to the feel, but since it is made of plastic, it must be called a lure. Today we see it modified with bodies and spoons into lures that are called "plug-worms," "spoon-worms," and "jig-worms." These combination lures are fished in the general manner of plugs, spoons, and jigs.

This chapter, however, is not about these combination lures, but instead specifically about the plastic worm with no accoutrements other than hooks. This is a deadly, deadly lure in deep water, especially when fished by a person who knows how to work it. But knowing how to work it is something special. In fact, when fishing with plastic worms everything is different.

You make your cast and allow the worm to sink to the bottom. This usually takes some waiting, for a plastic worm with just hooks will sink quite slowly. Properly made worms have enough buoyancy in the tail end to make the tail stand up and slowly undulate

Plastic worms can be fished in various combinations. From top to bottom: worm armed only with weedless hooks; worm with finned lead-head is popularly called jig-worm; worm with spoon is called spoon-worm, and worm with plug body and skirt is called plug-worm.

in the current. Let the worm rest on the bottom for a few seconds before making any reeling motions. When the retrieve is started, it is dead slow. Take a few turns on the reel handle and then pause a few seconds. A few more turns and another pause. Do this all the way back to the boat. It make take four or five minutes to fish out a long cast. Of course, when you get into a school of fish, you can expect to hook a fish on almost every cast and the fishing speeds up tremendously.

It takes a special skill to hook a fish on these worms. Rarely will bass sock them as they do with plugs and spoons. Instead the blacks pick them up by the tail and slowly inhale them. Obviously the "feel" of the plastic worm is so close to the real thing that bass don't regard them as foreign and spit them out. Bass strikes on these worms are usually felt in light "taps" relayed up the line. The reaction of a fellow not skilled in plastic worm fishing is to strike immediately to set the hook. This is wrong. All the quick-striker does is snatch the worm away from the fish.

Let the fish take the worm well into its mouth before ever raring back on the rod. My method is to immediately throw my reel into free spool. When line starts paying off the reel, I know the fish has the worm in its mouth and is moving off. Then—and only then —I sock-o the strike. If one is to hook fish with conventional plugs and spoons, he must set the hook as soon as the fish hits. If he waits or delays, he is almost certain to miss hooking the fish. It is the other way around with the plastic worm.

This manner of hooking fish on plastic worms is much easier described than done. It is quite difficult to overcome the habit of striking as soon as you feel the "tap." Unless you consciously keep your mind on it, you will be certain to strike too soon. It took a lot of plastic worm fishing trips for me to master the technique, and even now I occasionally will have a memory lapse and try to set the hook too soon.

After a bass is hooked on a plastic worm, the odds of losing the fish are slim. You will find the hooks almost always imbedded well inside the fish's mouth or even in the throat. Rarely are they just lip-hooked. If you do happen to bring in some that are lip-hooked, this is an indication that you are trying to set the hook a bit too soon.

The manner in which the worm is worked permits for some lazy fishing that can be highly productive when working a small lake or pond. Paddle to the up-wind side of the lake, cast out, and

allow the boat to drift across the lake. The drift will drag the worm
along the bottom at just about the right speed. When you get a
fish, just ease over the anchor and keep fishing the same spot. If
the spot fails to produce another fish, then resort to drifting again.

Texas lure fisherman, W. E. (Smokey) Stover with a pair of black bass
that fell victims to plastic worms.

Although plastic worm is deadly for black bass, it can also be a nuisance when small panfish abound. Author's son Carl exhibits a five-inch blue-gill that struck a plastic worm measuring six inches in length.

If survival in the wild hinged on a single lure, my choice would be the plastic worm. It is by no means an all-purpose lure, but it is one that will catch fish more consistently under all conditions than any other kind of hardware. This holds for fresh water fishing. If I had to survive on a single lure in salt water, it would be a toss-up between a spoon and a jig.

Although the plastic worm is a sure-fire deep water producer, it can at times be most effective along the shoreline and in shoal waters.

In the shallow water situation it is quite productive when brush, grass, and weeds rule out the use of underwater plugs and spoons. A plastic worm inched through grass can be pure poison, especially on bass during the spawning season.

There have been times when the only lure possible to use is the plastic worm. This occurs on small lakes choked with lily pads. On first glance these lakes may appear to have solid blankets of pads, but closer observation always reveals a lot of openings, maybe just a few feet in diameter. Use an unweighted worm armed with weedless hooks. Make your cast so the worm comes to rest atop the pads. Let it remain there a few seconds. Then slowly inch it across the pad. Do it in such a manner that part of the worm slips over the edge and into the water. Again wait a few seconds. Then inch it a bit more and let the worm slip off the pad and sink into the water. Quite often the water will explode with a bass smashing the worm just as it begins to sink.

If you don't get a strike at this point, just let the worm sink to the bottom and ease it through the pads. The weed guards will keep it from fouling. Worms fished in this manner have rewarded me with bass from under solid cover of lily pads. When fishing such dense cover, at least 20 pound test line must be used, even though the bass may only run in the two pound class. You must do a lot of horsing with the rod to pull fish out of the tangle.

The same fishing method can be used in working the worm in shallow water near the shoreline. Cast so that the worm lands on the bank a few inches from the edge of the water. Then inch it slowly to the water and allow it to drop in.

If the plastic worm has a disadvantage, it must be in its appeal to small fish. I don't mean small fish in the gamefish category. I mean those little panfish. It is most frustrating at times to be plagued with three and four inch bluegills hitting the worms. And these little rascals will strike plastic worms measuring six to eight

Flexible and pliable plastic has led to production of many life-like lures. From top to bottom: baitfish for offshore trolling; small minnow and squid; crawfish and shrimp, and small and large-size worms.

inches in length. A photo accompanying this chapter shows a youthful fisherman with a little bluegill caught on a six-inch plastic worm.

Use special care in the storage of all soft plastic lures. On some of the packages in which they come, you may read a line stating: "Safe to store in most plastic, painted or varnished containers." Note the word "most" is used. Apparently there is something used in the manufacture of some plastic containers, paints, and varnishes that makes them incompatible with soft plastic lures. The lures become gummy and will stick. Never store these lures in places that are subject to high temperatures over an extended period of time. They won't melt to liquid state, but they will "run" out of shape and become quite sticky. Take care in not getting any kind of oil or grease on them as these substances are likely to cause chemical changes. I once spilled a small bottle of insect repellent in a container with three or four plastic worms and ended up with a mass of colored jelly. Storage is best at room temperature. A friend once stored a package of plastic worms in his refrigerator for several

Introduction of pliable plastic into lure industry has led to life-like imitations of all kinds of aquatic life found around the typical fresh water lake or river. Above are frogs, crawfish, and bugs in various stages of their life span.

weeks. Not in the freezer compartment but in the regular food area. His worms became quite stiff and developed cracks.

The drawing at the end of this chapter shows two ways of rigging plastic worms to be weedless if you don't have weedless hooks available. In Fig. 1 the hook eye is forced through the body of the worm while the point and barb are lightly imbedded. The pressure of the fish biting down on the worm will force the point and barb to push out of the worm body and penetrate into the flesh of the fish's mouth. In Fig. 2 the plastic worm body is pushed over the entire shank of the hook. Then the worm body is S-curved and the hook point and barb are lightly imbedded. Again pressure from the bite will force the point and barb through the worm.

These two rigs are excellent for fishing shallow water and in weed and brush piles. The rigs are heavy enough for good casting distance with spinning or spin-cast gear. If additional casting distance is desired or one wants to get to the bottom quickly in deep water, a quarter-ounce ringed sinker can be attached to the hook eye with a line connector.

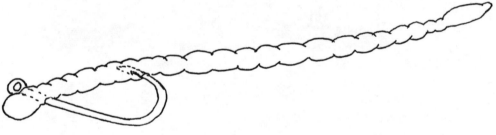

Fig. 1

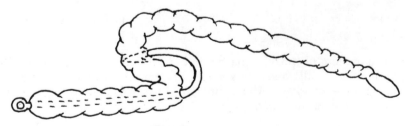

Fig. 2

11

FISHING THE JIGS

A hook with a lead body encased around a portion of its shank is called a jig. Because of its weight, compact size, and streamlined shape, it is the easiest of all artificial lures to cast. The lead bodies, which are called lead-heads, are molded on both straight-shanked and bent-shanked hooks. On those with straight shanks, the eye of the hook sticks out of the front of the lead-head, while on hooks with bent shanks, the eye sticks up through the top of the lead-head. In general trolling the jig with the eye straight out of the lead-head will ride a little shallower than the one with the eye coming out of the top of the lead-head.

The lead portions of the jigs, of course, are finished off in various colors. On small jigs the colors are solid, while on some large models, scale finishes are often applied. Jigs are further dressed up with rubber skirts, bucktails, nylon bristles, or feathers. These extend back partially covering or hiding the hook bend and point. Some are further implemented with propellers or spinners at the front. In the case of the plastic worm, the lure becomes a jig-worm when the body is threaded over the hook shank and butted against the lead-head.

Regardless of how the jig is dressed up, it is strictly an underwater lure. There is no way of fishing a jig on the surface unless it is trolled at high speed behind a boat—and at a speed like that the odds of getting a fish are nil. As soon as a jig hits the water, it sinks like a rock. If you want to get to the bottom fast—and especially so in fast-moving water—the jig is the lure to use.

The jig is fished in a manner implied by its name—jigging up and down. It is quite effective when you can make it dance a "lively jig" on the bottom. This is done by alternating a fast retrieve with a lot of rod tip popping. It can also be fished straight down under a boat drifting with the current or wind. The jig action is provided by erratically lifting and lowering the rod tip.

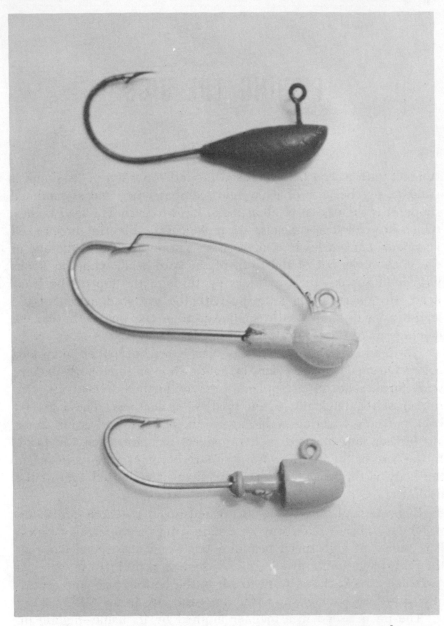

A few of the many shapes of lead-head jigs. One in center has wire guard on hook to make it weedless.

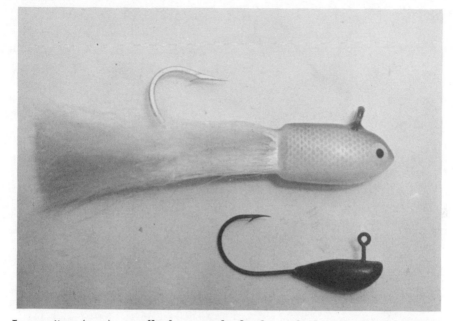

Large jigs (top) usually have scale finish applied to body. Small jigs (bottom) are finished in solid colors.

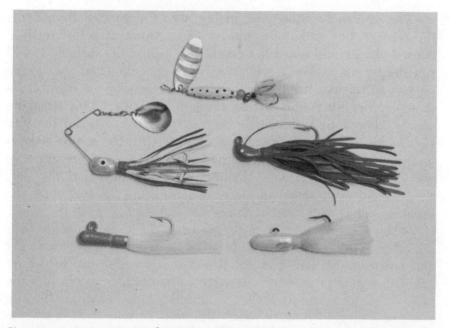

Jigs come in many combinations. Top to bottom: jig with leaf blade and bucktail is usually called a spinner; jig with spinner blade and rubber skirt and jig with weedless hook and rubber skirt; jigs with nylon bristles.

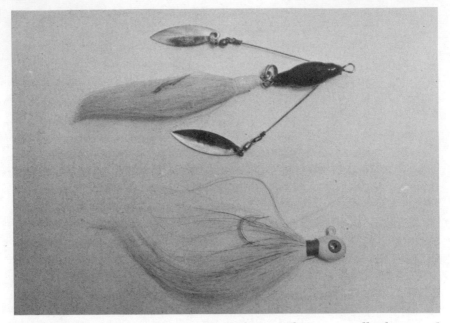

Jig at top has twin spinners. Jig at bottom has unusually long and flowing bucktail.

The jig can be fished reasonably near the surface by starting the retrieve the instant the lure hits the water. If a fast retrieve is used, the jig will ride five to eight feet below the surface. It will run deeper on a slower retrieve. Unlike the plug and spoon, the jig has no wiggle, wobble, or erratic movement of its own. On a steady retrieve it simply streaks through the water. This streaking can be altered by occasionally halting the retrieve to let the lure sink a little and then popping back sharply with the rod to make it jump up when the retrieve is started again. This is a very effective way of fishing in relatively shallow salt water bays and the surf. You can get extra action in the jig when fishing the surf since the breaking waves will cause it to tumble and dart.

When it comes to casting, the jig has a decided advantage over all other types of lures if fishing on a windy day. Its weight and compact size will give a fellow twice the distance he would get with a plug or spoon of the same weight when casting into the face of a strong wind. And when casting this same jig with the wind, a fellow can get "country mile" distance. This in itself is an advantage when it comes to fishing from the shoreline and the fisherman needs to reach water too deep to wade.

Small jigs can be fished suspended under popping floats. The manner is the same as when live bait is used, and this is to pop the float frequently by sharply twitching the rod tip. This in turn causes the suspended jig to jump up and down. A very popular fresh water white bass rig in the South consists of a small jig tied two to three feet behind a surface plug that has had all its hooks removed. The plug in this case plays a dual role of both float and teaser bait.

In trolling the jig is one of the most popular of lures. This is especially true in offshore salt water fishing. Its popularity in trolling stems from its marked advantage over plugs and spoons in that it rides steady and has no tendency to spin, regardless of the trolling speed. Consequently the headache of line twist is eliminated, and this in itself is a pleasure when one spends the entire day trolling. Personally when it comes to offshore trolling for fish like king mackerel, barracuda, bonita, etc., my choice is a large feathered jig or a jig with a large rubber skirt.

Jigs come in a wide range of sizes and weights ranging from ⅛th ounce up to one pound. The ⅛th ounce jig can be fished with

These are casting and trolling jigs. Top to bottom: jig with weedless hook and skirt for casting into weed beds and lily pads; medium-size trolling jig encased in plastic skirt; eight inch-long skirted jig with tandem hooks on beaded chain for offshore trolling.

ultra light spinning tackle on a windless day. I have not heard of
the one pound jig being used in American waters, but it is used to
some extent in deep water jigging in European and Japanese waters.

Although jigs are effective fish-getters, fishermen in general have
a tendency to push them to the sideline. I suspect that the jig's
lack of wiggle or wobble is the main reason so many anglers reject

Fresh water white bass such as these are particularly fond of striking
at jigs.

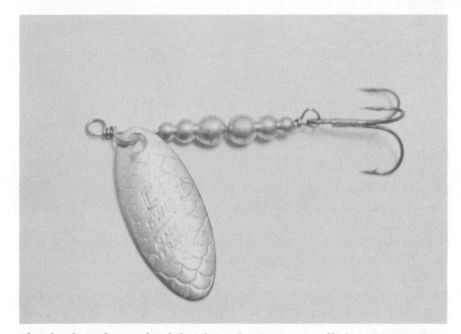

This hook with weighted beads and spinner is called a spinner. It is fished in same manner as jigs.

this lure. It deserves a better fate, and personally I recommend that no tackle box should be without a few jigs—if for no other reason than to have a lure that can be cast into a strong wind. One of the best white bass hauls I ever made was right below a central Texas dam on the Colorado River. I was fishing from the shoreline and there was no way to cast except into the face of a 25 to 30 mile per hour wind. I attempted to use plugs and spoons but because of the wind I could not reach the fast water where the fish were working. My salvation was a half-ounce black lead-head jig with white nylon bristles. It rewarded me with 25 white bass that morning.

The jig is also mighty handy when it comes to fishing fast-moving water or rapids since it is less likely than plugs and spoons to wedge in cracks or under rocks. When rigged with a weed guard, it is a good choice for fishing waters with heavy brush or lily pads.

12

SETTING THE HOOK

IN natural bait fishing a good many fish hook themselves with absolutely no assistance on the part of the fisherman. This is not true in lure fishing.

For the explanation we must go back to the construction of a fish's mouth, manner in which it uses its teeth, and manner in which it ingests its food.

Fish do not use their teeth for chewing up food as do humans. They use their teeth to grab, kill, and hold, and then they swallow whole whatever they are feeding upon. Except for certain predatory species such as sharks, barracuda, and the South American piranha, there are few fish that will attempt to grab and eat an object larger than itself. Sharks, barracuda, and piranha will attack large objects and tear off hunks of flesh. These chunks are then swallowed whole.

A fish normally takes its food by opening its mouth wide and "inhaling." The food comes into its mouth with the water "inhaled." As soon as the fish closes its mouth, this "inhaled" water is expelled out through its gills. The food meanwhile goes down its throat and into the stomach. Fish can "exhale" water just as readily as they can "inhale." If the food in the fish's mouth does not feel right, it will be "exhaled" immediately.

A natural bait impaled on a hook can feel right in a fish's mouth and be swallowed immediately. Throat muscles constricting on the bait force the hook barb to penetrate the fish's flesh. The fish is hooked and the fisherman didn't do a cotton picking thing to set the hook. Next time you fish with natural bait, note how many fish are hooked deep in the throat.

Artificial lures—except for those made of pliable plastic or rubber—have a foreign feel in a fish's mouth. When a fish feels the hard object in its mouth, it will exhale the lure. Unless a hook snags a lip on the way out, the fish is lost. Consequently if an angler is to be successful with lures, he must do something to remedy the situation. This something is snapping back the rod tip. This does not jerk the lure away from the fish as one might suppose, but it causes the trebel hooks on the lure to flip wide. That tail hook in particular flips up and usually strikes flesh in the roof of the fish's mouth or the fish's top lip. Make notes on your next few fishing trips and you will discover that most fish taken on lures are snagged by the tail hook—imbedded in the upper part of the fish's mouth or lip.

The fish's ability to "exhale" objects that don't feel right is the reason very few lures are ever imbedded deep in the fish's mouth or in its throat. This is true with hard lures. Deep mouth or throat hooking is rather common with soft, pliable lures. Their feel is right and consequently the fish attempt to swallow them.

Let me relate some tests I made at the Wildlife Kingdom Fishing Resort near Newton in east Texas. I picked this particular resort because one of the lakes has a pier from which children do a lot of worm fishing for bluegills and crappie. They have baited up the water so much that fish hang around in large numbers and move up plainly visible in the water. This made the tests easy because I could observe closely what was happening.

I made the tests with bits of real worms, bits of plastic worms and tiny hard-bodied flies. No action whatsoever was imparted in the use of any of these baits. The fish inhaled the bits of real worms and frequently hooked themselves deep in their throats. Then I put on bits of real worms that had been dabbed with a drop of oil, petroleum oil which is foreign to fish. The fish "inhaled" the bits, but the taste was foreign and they immediately "exhaled" the worms. A few stupid oafs hooked themselves in the lips when they "exhaled" and tried to turn away at the same time.

The identical results were obtained when I used bits of plastic worms. The feel was "right" in the mouths of the fish and consequently they swallowed and hooked themselves. Plastic bits with machine oil were "inhaled" and then immediately "exhaled." Again a few fish lip-hooked themselves in making fast turns on the "exhale." Perhaps fear was aroused in these fish and caused them to make the too-quick getaway turns.

Results of tests with the hard-bodied flies were startlingly different. The flies were taken readily enough because they looked like something good to eat. But their "feel" inside the fishes' mouths was foreign—and the flies were immediately "exhaled." Again a few were lip-hooked when they made those fast getaway turns. When I started jerking the line as soon as a fish mouthed a fly, I started catching the little rascals almost every time. One morning I ran 17 straight before suffering a miss.

These tests provided the obvious answer. If you are to be successful in lure fishing, you have to do your part—and that part is more than just imparting a tantilizing lure action to attract the fish. You must keep wide awake and do your part, too, in setting the hook. This isn't lazy man fishing, so don't expect the fish to do everything for you. Remember it takes two to tango.

Setting the hook will vary from species to species. With some the strike must be gentle. With others it must be sharp and solid. The kind of strike necessary depends upon how tough or tender the flesh of the mouth is. For example, use just wrist action in setting the hooks on members of the salt water weakfish clan. This clan includes speckled trout, white trout, sand trout, and silver trout. All have one thing in common—tender mouths that tear easily.

Use the "sock it to 'em" strike in bedding hooks in hard-mouthed fish. A few such species are striped bass, redfish, ling, king mackerel, barracuda, bonita, and dolphin in salt water, and black bass, lake trout, muskellunge, walleyes, and northern pike in fresh water.

Fish are easiest to hook on trolled lures. Next easiest in hooking comes on underwater lures. Hooking is toughest when strictly surface lures are used.

The trolled lure is moving through the water when the fish hits it. It is also moving at a steady and fast enough clip to drive the hook points and barbs home when they strike the solid flesh in a fish's mouth. Sure there are times when fish strike trolled lures and are not hooked. But these times are in the decided minority. I have never kept catch figures on trolled lures, but I would guess-estimate that out of every ten strikes, nine fish are hooked. I don't mean that all nine fish will be landed because some may only be lip-hooked, and in horsing fish so hooked it is almost a certainty that the hook will be torn out of the flesh.

Again I will have to guess-estimate on hookings when strikes are made on underwater lures. In this case I would estimate that three of every five strikes result in hooked fish. As in the case of the trolled lure, the underwater lure is moving when it is hit. The difference in the number of hookings is a result of the difference in the retrieve speeds. The normal—even fast—retrieve used in casting is considerably slower than the speed of the lure trolled behind the boat. Consequently this means that if the caster is to

hook his fish, he will have to do something on his own part. He
must strike—or snap back the rod—to bed the hook.

In short, the fish taken on the trolled lure hooks itself. The
fisherman does nothing. In fact, quite frequently the rod is stuck
in a rod-holder during the course of the troll. The fisherman takes
over only after the strike and when he has a fish hooked. In the
case of the caster, he must strike in order to give the hooks that
extra drive necessary to penetrate flesh.

Now to hooking fish on the surface plug. If you expect the fish
to do all the work and hook itself, then be prepared to accept something like an average of one hooked fish for every 12 to 15 strikes.
If you get with it and do your part, the average should be closer
to one fish out of every five strikes. Several top notch pros tell me
that one fish hooked out of every three strikes on a surface plug
is darned good. This is an average covering a number of fishing
trips. There will be times when you hook a fish on every cast on
a surface plug. These are unusual occasions such as when a huge
school of fish goes on a mad feeding spree or with black bass during the spawning season when they will attack with a vengence
anything that comes near their nest.

There are several reasons when it is more difficult to hook fish
on surface plugs. To begin with many of the strikes are made when
the plug is absolutely motionless. Even more important is the
manner in which the fish strike. In the case of the trolled and
underwater lure, the fish grabs at the entire lure. The picture is
different when surface lures are involved. Fish are more wary of
surface objects than underwater objects. Remember the fish sees
the surface object as a dark silhouette. Under normal circumstances
the fish approaches the surface lure with caution, and then when
it decides to strike does so more by nipping than by outright grab-
bing. The exception is with flies and bugs which are very small in
size.

This nip at a surface plug is a rattlesnake-fast strike in which
the fish bites down on a part of the lure and quickly releases it.
It is almost like the sailfish that whacks a bait first with its bill to
kill and then circles back around to mouth it as it sinks helplessly
in the water. I have long believed that the lure manufacturer who
is able to come up with a surface plug that will suddenly lose buoy-
ance when struck and sink like a dying minnow will make a fortune.

All of this means that if a fellow is to be consistently successful
with top water lures, he must stay alert and fish at fishing. He must

watch his plug all the time. At times when the water is calm and
clear and the light is right, he will be able to see the fish working
up slowly beneath the plug. This is a tense, tense moment. He must
resist the urge to hurry up and strike, for if he strikes too soon, he
will certainly snatch the lure away from the fish and possibly spook
the fish. He must time his strike to coincide with the split second
that the plug starts to "act crazy on its own. If he waits too long,
he is bound to miss the fish.

Even after the fish is hooked, the fish that struck the surface
plug stands a better chance to win its freedom than does the one
hooked on an underwater plug. Remember the fish that hits underwater is likely to have the entire lure in its mouth with both sets
of gang hooks bedded in flesh. The one that hits the surface plug
is more apt to be hooked only by a single set of gang hooks and
quite frequently only by a single tine. Furthermore the fish hitting
the surface plug is more apt to jump and tail-walk on the surface.
This gives the fish a better chance to throw the plug.

Personally I get a tremendous thrill out of catching fish on surface plugs. Seeing the strike and the explosion of water when the
fish is hooked is truly a sight to behold. The sound of the splash is
something akin to that made when a guy falls overboard. I can
get a bigger thrill out of catching one fish on a surface plug than
catching five on underwater runners.

If you are fishing to eat, then the better choice would be an
underwater lure.

Hooks on all lures should be kept surgical needle-sharp. Dull
hooks will work on trolled lures and to some extent will catch fish
on underwater runners. But the dull hook will get you nothing if
it is on a surface plug. With top water lures you need all the hook
sharpness and penetration you can get to nail your fish.

If the lure is the type with a rubber skirt covering the hook,
check to see if a hook is actually on the lure. Just a few weeks before I started this chapter I made a bass fishing trip to a small lake.
I had five solid strikes but no fish. I was quite embarrassed when
I checked the lure and found no hooks—and it was a brand new
lure. When I looked back into the plastic container, I found a pair
of two-tined hooks. Then when I got around to reading the fine
print on the box, I learned the lure came with two hooks—one
silver plated and the other gold plated. The angler had the option
of using the finish he desired. The exasperating thing about it all
was that when I put hooks on the lure—either silver or gold—I got

no more strikes. This does not mean that the hooks upset the action of the lure. It was simply a case of the fish moving out of the area. Much later in the day—and with the same lure—I got back into bass.

On another occasion some years earlier I had a different experience. I caught three or four bass and then had plenty of good strikes but no fish hooked. Upon examination of the lure I discovered the single tined hook had been bent straight. In between the fish caught and the many strikes and no fish, I had snagged a log. In pulling the lure free from the snag I had straightened out the hook, but since it was covered with a rubber skirt, I did not notice it. It pays to check hooks regularly for either broken or straightened out tines.

I don't mind weed guards on underwater lures, but I don't like to use them on surface plugs because of the manner in which the fish strike. Use of the surface plug in waters with lily pads, floating logs and timber stands calls for extremely accurate casting. Then with skillful rod manipulation you can work the plug around the snags without fouling up even if no weed guards are used. This accurate casting and rod manipulation can mean the difference between fish and an empty stringer.

13

PLAYING THE FISH

ONE might suppose that a fish lure-hooked is fighting for its freedom at a greater disadvantage than the fish snagged on a plain hook. Once in a while this is true, but in the majority of the cases the lure-hooked fish has better odds of escaping—especially if the rod is in hands unskilled in artificial lure fishing. This might frighten some folks away from using lures. I feel, however, that it also presents a challenge that should cause a lot of folks to go in for lure angling . . . if for no other reason than to prove to themselves and the world that they are more skilled anglers than bait fishermen.

Whether the lure is a plug or spoon, it is something that gives a fish leverage in its fight for freedom. When a fish scraps to free itself of the hook, it is not always a matter of a steady pull. The fish frequently will shake its head violently to free itself of the stinging hook. In bait fishing the bait is either swallowed, torn off the hook, or shaken off the hook. This means the fish is fighting to rid itself of a bare hook, which has very little weight. Head-shaking alone will not throw the hook. The bare hook that comes free of the fish does so because it is ripped through the flesh, or a large hole is worn in the flesh and the hook simply falls out when the angler allows slack in the line.

Lures, too, will rip out of flesh. This usually happens when the angler allows slack in the line at the same time when the fish violently shakes its head. The weight of the lure, which is considerably more than that of a bare hook, gives the fish leverage. That big lure flops back and forth during the head-shaking and unless a strain is maintained on the line it will quickly wear a hole in the flesh and the hook will fall free. If the fish happens to be shaking its head on slack line and the angler tightens up during the course of the shaking, the lure is almost certain to tear out of the flesh.

A fish is toughest to keep hooked when it fights on the surface. This lake trout has just pitched lure free from its mouth because author tried to take photo and fish at same time with the result being he failed to maintain tension on line.

Fish are tough to keep on when they start tailwalking on the surface. Note this tarpon is still hooked, but the small fish used as bait has been thrown up the leader. Tailwalkers can throw lures just as easily. (Florida Development Commission Photo)

The most spectacular fight a fish can put up is above the surface of the water—jumping, gray-hounding, and tail-walking. And
this is where it is easiest to lose a lure-hooked fish. A slack line will
almost always lead to the fish flinging the lure back at you. Too
much tension on the line will often result in the line or leader part-
ing when the fish hits the water. How much or how little tension
you maintain on the line is something that comes through fishing
experience.

If this bit about leverage and shaking out hooks sounds foreign,
try this little experiment with a fish you have just landed. Bed a
hook, free of line or strain, in its mouth. No matter how vigorously
you shake that fish, you won't shake the hook out. Do the same
thing with a line and strain on the hook, and you will discover
repeated shaking will cause the hook to wear a large hole in the
flesh and it will drop out when there is no line tension. Take a
plug or spoon and bed it in a fish's lips and then shake the fish. The
leverage of the swinging lure will cause the hook to wear a large
hole in the flesh—and there goes the lure sailing off into space.
The same lure with too much line tension during the course of the
fish shaking will cause the hook to tear flesh and then fall out
when the tension is released.

The artificial lures fish have the most difficulty in throwing are
those with weed-guards. These are the "weedless" or "snag-proof"
plugs and spoons. It works on the "safety pin" principle. When the
fish bites down on the lure, the spring wire that protects the hook
point from weeds and snags releases and bends down. Once the
fish is hooked, this same piece of wire tends to spring back to its
former position. If the fish is lip-hooked, the wire guard can spring
back to act like a "safety pin." This will prevent the hook from
falling out of a hole worn into the flesh. It will not, however, prevent flesh tearing which can be caused by too much tension on
the line.

There is just one trouble with these "weedless" lures. They may
keep a lure free of weeds and snags, but their hooks are more
difficult to bed in a fish's mouth. I use "weedless" lures only when
absolutely necessary. I know some anglers who would not use
them on a bet. Their pet complaint is "a weedless lure is a fishless
lure." I won't go to that extreme, although no one will ever convince me that it is as easy to hook a fish on a weedless lure as on
a conventional one.

Biologists claim that a fish's brain is so small and under-developed that it is insensitive to pain. I won't dispute his claim because in closed tank experiments I have caught the same fish over and over again within the space of a few minutes. Man, however, is quite sensitive to pain, and a lure with all its bright, dangling gang or treble hooks is a deadly weapon. It is a weapon that fish frequently use unconsciously and without premeditation to inflict nasty wounds on fishermen.

Louisiana outdoor writer Mike Cook keeps tension on rod even while guide grabs fish. Tension is important to keep fish from throwing lure free.

Jesse Lewis of Newton, Texas, shows how to land black bass by lipping the fish. Fish is grasped firmly on lower lip and then brought into boat in sweeping motion.

This calls for discretion when it comes to landing a lure-hooked fish. I have seen many fish shake so violently on the floor of a boat that they threw plugs or spoons into angler's hands, arms, or legs. In handling a fish in the boat, run your hand down the leader and get a firm grip on the front of the lure. Then if the fish does shake it free, it will not go flying through the air and end up in someone's anatomy.

Lure-hooked fish should always be landed with a landing net. The netting will tangle a lure enough so that it can't be pitched into your arm. If the fish is too large for a net, then use a gaff hook.

I used to fish with a fellow who prided himself on leading black bass up to the boat and then reaching over and lifting them aboard by gripping the lower lip. During this process he always held his rod tip high to maintain tension on the line. This is the correct thing to do. But then there came the day when just as he reached to lip the fish, it shook its head vigorously. The lure ripped free and smashed into the fisherman's face. One hook bedded in his

Best way to land fish in lure fishing is with landing net. It can protect angler from flying plugs. (Johnson Motors photo)

cheek and another in his ear. Only his glasses saved his eyes, but even then he lost his glasses overboard because they were knocked off by the force of the plug.

The only safe way to remove a fish from the water is with landing net or gaff hook. Or if it is small enough, you can pick it aboard with the line.

14

THE WINDOW DRESSINGS

LURE finishes are a lot like women's dress styles—they can cover up a lot of faults and sins. I always feel sorry for the Joe who goes for a gal because of the styles she wears. Usually—too late—he learns he has latched on to a scatterbrain, dullard, or simply a pig in a poke.

It is much the same way with some lures, and as far as I am concerned some of the beautiful finishes applied are more window dressing than anything else. Frequently the finishes catch far more fishermen than fish. I am not really knocking this—because if a lure is to catch fish, it must first catch the fisherman. The point I am making is that too frequently fishermen become overly enthusiastic about the lure finish and completely overlook the action, which in the final analysis is what activates the fish into striking.

Let's start out with the floating plugs. Until the mid-1950s almost every floating plug made was white or light colored on the bottom. The top and upper sides were authentically finished to resemble a minnow, frog, etc. The bottoms, however, were invariably light. These light colored bottoms—or bellies—are correct as far as nature is concerned. All fish, wildlife, and birdlife are lighter in color on the bellies than on the sides and backs.

But did you ever consider how the floating plug looks to a fish beneath it? Remember the sky is providing the light, and the lure is between the fish and source of light. Consequently the lure appears only as a dark silhouette. Even a snowball with a strong light behind it appears dark. All those beautiful back and side markings mean nothing to the fish since the fish can't distinguish them anyway. Frankly I can't see much use of fancy patterns whatsoever on strictly floating lures. Unless the fish has a flashlight, the lure will appear only as a silhouette. I maintain that the effectiveness of floating lures depends on two things—the action and whatever fish-attracting sounds the lure can be made to imitate.

To prove this point I have consistently caught a wide assortment of fresh water fish on surface plugs that had the finishes completely scraped off.

Lure finish, however, does come into play when the plug is one that works underwater. This lure can be seen more plainly by the fish, and there are no ripples to diffuse the light nor distort the shape or size of the lure. Once a lure goes beneath the surface, its colors become visible to the fish. The vividness of these colors depend upon two things—clarity of the water and depth at which the lure is being fished.

In gin clear water use plugs with somewhat subdued patterns and colors. If you go for red or yellow on your plugs, use normal reds and yellows and not the neon or fluorescent ones. This is especially true in fresh water fishing where the most productive retrieve is a slow one. Most fresh water fish eyeball a lure for some time before striking. The action of the lure captures their attention. Then comes the pause in the retrieve. If the finish or color is too bright, the fish is likely to recognize it as something phony and veer off. Remember there are fewer species of fish competing for food in a fresh water lake or stream than in the open sea. Consequently fresh water fish seem to feed much more leisurely.

What holds true for the gaudy plug in clear water also holds for the metal spoon. There is such a thing as too much flash. Most of the better spoon fishermen use spoons with dull or satin finishes in extremely clear water. They turn to the real flashers when the water is off-color.

The deeper the lure—plug or spoon—sinks, the more flash it needs. Remember that water filters light, and the deeper the water, the less light penetrating. As a result the lure fished deep merely becomes a shadow that is visible from only quite close range. In extremely deep water lure color or finish means little. Even the flash of a spoon is reduced because there is so little light.

All bottom bumping lures have one thing in common. They are either made of materials that will wiggle or have some sort of attachments that will wiggle, spin or flutter in the slightest of currents or rod manipulation on the part of the fisherman. Bodies are usually made of flexible plastic or rubber, and the attachments are plastic or rubber skirts, small propellers or spinner blades, or frizzy bucktails.

Some colors retain distinction at greater depths than others. Colors that can be distinguished best under water are white, red and yellow. Others lose definition at rather shallow depths. Yet this does not mean colors such as blue, green, purple or black are valueless. Quite to the contrary. Minnows swim close to the surface and in shallow water. They are found in varying shades of blue, green, purple and black. A lure fished at minnow depth—or in shallow water—should have a color and finish to resemble the minnows that inhabit the waters in which you fish. These finishes are important if the lure is an underwater one. If it is strictly a surface lure, finish really means little since when a fish views it from below, it appears only as a silhouette.

Consider, for example, the number of fresh water plugs made to resemble frogs. Some are strictly surface lures. Others are designed to work a few feet below the surface. All come with authentic frog finishes. I have yet to see a silver or gold frog. I suppose some have been made, but if they are great fish-getters, then some manufacurer is losing his shirt by keeping it a secret. And I have not met a lure manufacturer yet who did not boom his latest creation or finish as the greatest fish-catcher since the invention of the hook itself.

One lure maker—I won't use his name in order to protect his business—wrote me the following in answer to questions about finishes:

"I have 27 color patterns and finishes for each of the 10 lures my company makes. Truthfully there are many finishes I would not use for my fishing. I have to supply these finishes because they are what fishermen want, and if I am to remain in business, I must cater to the whims of these buyers. This is a hazardous business that rises and falls on the tastes of fishermen. A lure can become a success overnight and it can die just as fast. Every time you see a store advertising lures for half or one-third their retail price, you can figure the store is trying to get rid of dead lures."

With one exception I can vouch for what the man writes. I feel he is incorrect in describing the lures with cut rate prices as being "dead lures." As far as I am concerned a lure never dies. I would rather refer to the cut-rate price ones as "displaced" or "replaced" models. Sort of like Ford's automobiles. There was the Model T. It was replaced by the Model A, which in time again was replaced by the V-8 and so forth. The old ones still work, but they just are not as efficient as the newer models. What happens in the automobile or airplane industry—or in business—also happens in making lures. It is a story of displacement, replacement and retirement, and it is something we must learn to live with.

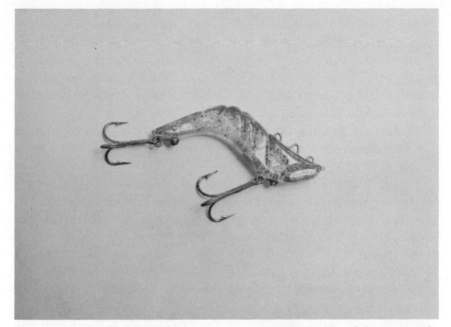

This rigid plastic shrimp has little eye appeal to the fisherman. The lure, a Plugging Shorty Shrimp, is one of the most effective fish-getters on the Texas coast. This is one of the author's favorites for speckled trout fishing.

Folks who read the writings of outdoors writers follow them like hawks for one of four reasons—(1) to get their names in the papers, (2) to badger free hunting and fishing trips, (3) to learn more about outdoors sports, and (4) to attempt to show the outdoor writer up as a fraud. Consequently a writer can not go around indiscriminately recommending every lure he receives for field testing. Wild recommendations may get him a lot of free lures, but it will lose him a lot of readers.

Let me cite a couple of experiences with field testing lures.

I was not particularly enthused about the appearance of some sample lures sent to me. The lure was a rigid plastic shrimp and amber in color. The manufacturer sent me a half dozen, all the same color. I kept two and gave four away to fellows who fished lures. I left my lures in the tackle box and stuck with proven lures. Meanwhile three of the fellows to whom I gave lures tested them religiously and in the space of a week had excellent results. They passed the word around, adding, of course, that I also used this particular lure. The plug in the space of a few weeks became a tremendous success on the upper Texas coast, and the manufacturer gave me a lot of credit for making his product click in my area.

But I did it in a back-handed way that was not fair to the maker. I should have tested it immediately as did my friends to whom I had given lures. This particular lure has been a consistent speckled trout catcher on the Texas coast for 20 years now. I like its action and I love to fish it, but I still contend it has little appeal to the eye of a fisherman.

Then there was the time when I almost gave a good reputation to a beautifully finished plug that eventually turned out to be a terrible dud.

It took place on a speckled trout trip. Whenever I go fishing I take two or three rods and reels all rigged for immediate action. On this particular trip I had two—one rigged with a gold spoon and the other with this beautiful plug. I caught several dozen specks on the spoon and then lost it on a snag. I would have started using the plug except for the fact that I did not like the build-up and movement of a summer squall. So I headed back to the boat basin without ever wetting the plug.

The fishing camp operator at the basin was a great one for getting on the phone and notifying the local radio stations on who caught what, where and on what kind of bait. The operator noted my catch and while I was loading the boat on the trailer, she got on the phone. When I went back to buy a pack of smokes, I was just in time to straighten out the mess. She had seen my fish, counted them, and then noted that beautiful lure hanging on the rod. She had assumed the fish were caught on the lure.

Lure anglers are an interesting breed. All that is necessary is for them to see one good string of fish taken on a lure. Then they all want to run out and buy one just like it.

15

HOW BIG, HOW MANY

GENERALLY speaking big fish take big lures and small fish take small hardware. This, however, is not a hard and fast rule. If it was, then there would be no explanation for trout and salmon being caught on small flies or black bass hitting tiny popping bugs.

A cautiousness on the part of the fish, I believe, is the main reason most large fish are caught on big lures and small fish on small ones.

Big fish get to be big fish because they are cautious—and don't make foolish mistakes. Although they will hit a bait or lure with a mighty smash, they are inclined to study the offering at some length before making their play. The exception comes when a school is composed entirely of big fish. Then they lose much of their caution and charge right in almost recklessly.

Small fish—unless they are extremely hungry—don't attack objects too large to swallow. Remember fish don't chew their food. They swallow it whole. Consequently one does not often catch yearling bass on plugs measuring six inches or more in length. Those taken on big lures are mainly ones making playful passes. Note that a good percentage of small fish caught on big lures are done so because of hooks fouling in their bodies rather than in the mouths. Small fish are much more reckless in their feeding than are large fish. The small fellows appear to compete with each other in getting to a small lure or bait first. The larger fish in a school seem more content to lurk off-stage or in the wings.

A general rule in lure fishing is that the more turbid the water, the larger the lure needed. This is obvious for if the lure is to be seen by the fish, it must be visible. The large lure can be seen from a greater distance than the small one. The size of lure used in this situation will be dictated by the water fished. For example, consider small pond fishing. Before ever fishing the pond, try to determine from other anglers the approximate size fish in it. If the

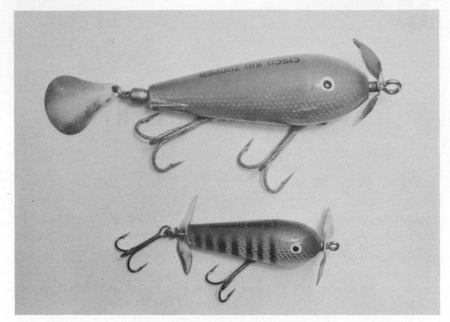

Two sizes of Cisco Kid Topper lures. Plug at top is suitable for surf and salt water fishing. Bottom one can be handled on light tackle.

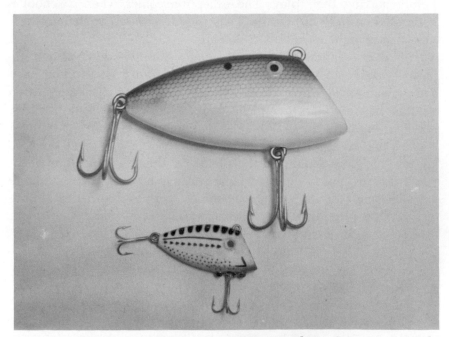

Two sizes of Whopper Stopper's Bayou Boogie plugs. One at top weighs three ounces and is for salt water fishing.

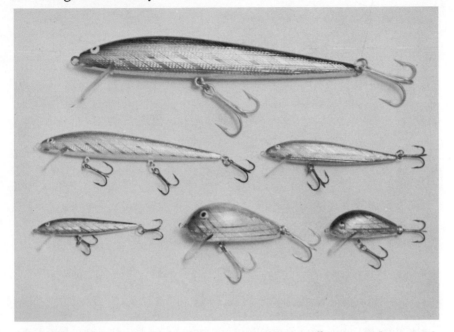

Some lures like the Rebel come in many sizes, offering angler a wide range in fishing.

pond is known to contain few or no fish in excess of two or three pounds in size, then go with artificials about one or two inches in length when the water is clear. When the water is off-color, then use lures three to four inches in length. The six to eight inch lures would be useless because they would be too big for the fish involved. Now switch over to the salt water situation. Suppose you are wade-fishing in water two to three feet deep. The two to three inch lures would be right for clear conditions, with the four to six inchers appropriate for off-color conditions. Use of the foot long offshore lure will only get you a sore arm—from casting.

Another general rule to follow is that lure size can be increased as the water depth increases. The exception comes when you know a body of water contains no large fish.

I have four tackle boxes. Three are stocked for fresh water fishing and one for salt water. On the surface this would seem to indicate that I do most of my fishing in fresh water. This is not true at all. Actually my salt water trips outnumber my fresh water trips around eight to one. My collection of lures accumulated over some 30 years numbers around 2,000. They represent a small fortune, but most were given to me as professional samples for field

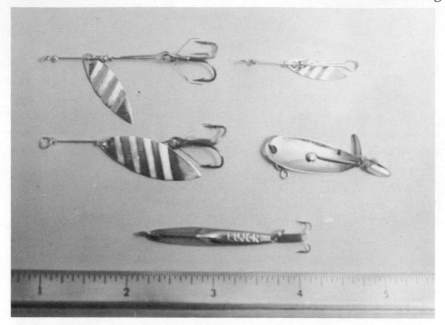

These spinners and spoons are light enough to be handled on very light spinning tackle. They are quite effective in still, quiet water.

testing. This is one of the fringe benefits of being an outdoors writer. In my collection the fresh water models outnumber the salt water lures by about three to one. Obviously I could not cram all 2,000 lures into the four boxes even if I melted the stuff down and poured it in.

Before each fishing trip I go through a sorting process of shelving some lures and replacing them in the tackle box with different models. Relatively little time is spent doing this in the salt water box. On salt water fishing trips my box contains about a dozen models and colors that are proven fish-getters—plus another half dozen models that I may desire to field test. If I am not interested in field testing on a particular trip, then I just go out with the dozen or so proven lures.

When I go on a fresh water trip, I usually take two tackle boxes—one crammed with two or three dozen proven fish-getters, and the other filled with two or three dozen field test models and "exotics." I call some lures "exotics" because they are such strange looking contraptions and look like nothing a self respecting fish would want to feed on. If my trip is an extended one of perhaps a week and especially to a small lake of say less than 50 acres in size, then I take along a third tackle box with more "exotics."

If I had to buy lures with my hard earned money, I would stock my salt water box with about a dozen proven lures and forget all about the "exotics." My fresh water box would include two dozen proven lures and a dozen "exotics." Lure prices range from around 50 cents for lead-head jigs to $3.50 for big offshore gamefish plugs and spoons. The cost for stocking the salt water box would run around $20 to $25. The average fresh water fisherman won't face a situation of having to buy big offshore lures, so the cost of stocking his box would range $40 to $45.

I think all fish have the ability to learn, if not by reason at least by association. Most species when they encounter a bad experience are not apt to go for a repeat performance immediately. With some species like the black bass and fresh water trout, this retention of knowledge gained through association can last for quite some time. And this can be most frustrating to the bass fisherman working a small lake. The blacks get used to seeing the same lures day after day and through association they learn these lures can make them poor insurance risks. When I fish a small lake, I start using the old standbys on the assumption that the body of water

At quick glance these lures look alike. Top is Cordell Hot Spot, an underwater plug that sinks medium fast. Bottom is Cordell Gay Blade, a deep water runner that sinks like a rock.

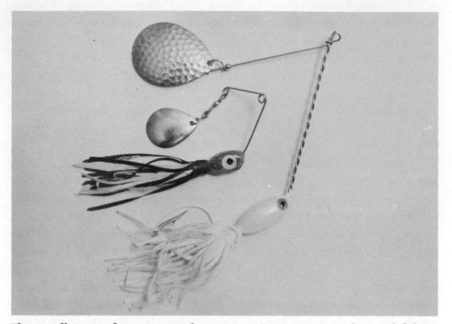

The small jig and spinner is for casting. Larger one is for surf fishing and trolling.

Some fish like the lake trout above prefer large lures. This 30-inch laker hit a spoon measuring six inches in length.

has not been fished hard. If I know it has been fished real hard, then I use the new field test models and the "exotics." I have had remarkable luck doing this, and I have enlisted the aid of a number of companions to prove the point. We would fish from the same boat. One of us would use the old standbys, while the other would work the "exotics." There were many trips when the standbys produced nothing, while the "exotics" paid off handsomely. This explains how some "exotics" get such fantastic reputations in fresh water fishing.

Salt water fish are not restricted to an area such as the case with fresh water fish. Even the non-migratory salt water species move from bay to bay or from bay to open sea or vice versa. Consequently the odds of them running afoul the same lure time after time are rather remote. Furthermore through years of experience, I have found salt water fish are far less apt to hit "exotics" than are fresh water species. Salt water fish show a decided preference for lures that resemble something upon which they naturally feed.

All of this leads up to another general rule for lure fishing. A greater variety of lures is needed for fresh water fishing than in salt water, and the smaller the body of fresh water, the more "exotics" necessary. I trust this answers the question that is so often put to me: "How many lures should I have in my tackle box?"

The time of the day or night plays a part in lure size. A good rule of thumb to follow is to use large lures at night or on days when the sky is dark or heavy overcast. When the light is bright, small lures will do the trick. To further complicate matters, always keep in mind water turbidity. If the sky is bright but the water is off-color, then you should go with large lures.

16

LURE LIFE

AN artificial lure—in addition to being effective as a fish-getter—is "deathless" and is the most inexpensive of all fishing baits. The "deathless" and "most inexpensive" go hand in glove. Let me explain by comparing a lure with live bait. Whatever the live bait—worm, shrimp, minnow, crawdad, etc.—it is good for one fish, occasionally two. If the first fish you catch does not kill the live bait, the second one is certain to do so. Fish may take a lure away from you by breaking the leader, but they can't kill a lure. Consequently the same lure can be used over and over again. The same lure will catch fish until it is lost, borrowed, or stolen. This might run into hundreds of fish. No live shrimp, minnow, worm, etc., can substantiate a similar claim.

Live bait is good for one trip. That which is not used can't be kept alive—except in the case of worms—for a fishing trip a week later. The lure, however, is good for trip after trip. This is what makes the lure so inexpensive. A good lure depending upon its size ranges in price from 50 cents to $3.50. Every time you purchase live bait, even in the case of the lowly worms, you spend right around $2. If you make 20 trips using live bait, your bait cost hits $40. A $2 lure used on 20 trips averages out to 10 cents a trip.

That $40 spent on live bait can be put to good use at the lure counter and you can stock up on enough lures to carry you through several years of fishing. In fact, they could carry you a lifetime if you led enough of a charmed life to miss hanging up on snags and tangling with fish too frisky for your tackle. But fishing is like every gamble in life—you can't win a thing unless you are willing to risk occasional losses.

Barring loss to a snag or big fish—or some forgetful borrower—a lure is "deathless" as long as you give it reasonable care and maintenance. This means the care you show it after fishing trips and in the tackle box.

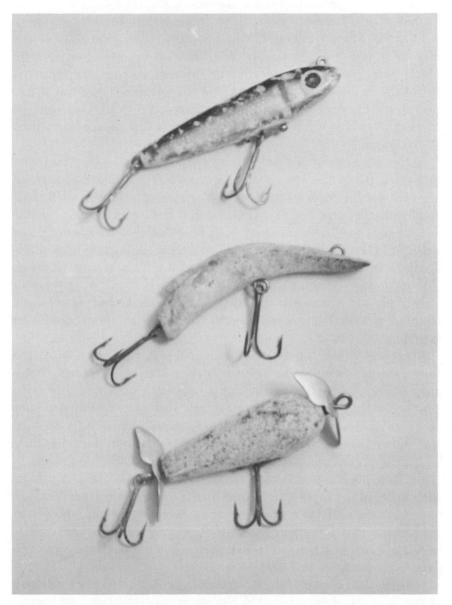

Above is example of what can happen to plugs if stored wet. These
plugs are covered with mold. Since finishes are fused into plastic bodies,
these plugs can be restored to almost new condition with soapy water
and wire kitchen pot cleaner.

Lures fished in fresh water require a minimum of upkeep. Just make sure they are free of bits of weed and are dry when stored. Frequently test hook points for sharpness.

Salt water, however, is rough on lures. Before the lure is stored, it must be washed thoroughly in fresh water to remove all traces of salt. If you don't, then expect to see rust or corrosion form on metal parts, and a strange kind of mildew on the lure finish. A metal spoon stored for a long period with traces of salt on it can be ruined. Corrosion is certain to eat away the luster and pit the metal badly. This won't happen if the lure is first cleaned and then stored properly.

Most lures today are sold in small plastic boxes. Yet so many fishermen dump the lures into the trays in their tackle boxes and give the plastic boxes to their wives for storing needles and thread. Really that plastic box is a natural for lure storage—even inside the tackle box. They are good insurance for the unexpected. For example, there was the time when a fellow fishing with me suddenly shifted his weight and overturned the boat in a small river. My tackle box—a metal one—was open but all of my lures were in closed plastic containers. I lost the tackle box, but the plastic containers floated and I recovered almost all of them along the shoreline.

The plastic lure boxes must be clean and dry when lures are stored in them. Otherwise look for rust or corrosion to form. Some anglers line the bottom of the containers with pieces of oily rags. This is okay as long as the oil is a fish oil. Stay away from petroleum oils and products since their taste and smell are foreign to fish. Fish oils, however, are attractive to fish, although the odor may be a little unpleasant on your nostrils.

In this connection I had one humorous experience. A fellow with little fishing experience asked me to make a trip with him. He quite frankly said he wanted to learn more about the sport and warned me that he would ask a million questions. That was okay with me, because I happen to like inquisitive people. It shows they have both initiative and ambition.

On the first day of the trip we caught fish until they ran out of our ears. My host attributed the great success to me. Modestly (?) I did not contradict him. He showered me with attention, and quite frankly I was enjoying it and soaking up the praise like a tissue absorbs water. The real truth of the matter is that it was one of those days when the fish hit any and everything. My host would have cleaned up on fish even if we had never met. That night he industriously cleaned all the rods and reels—mine too—and even got into the tackle boxes. Meanwhile I was enjoying television and a bent elbow. It took him about an hour to do these chores, and when he returned to the cabin, he announced everything was clean, including "oiling the lures."

I almost choked on my drink asking what he meant by "oiling the lures."

"Oh, I sprayed them with this to keep them from rusting," he said proudly holding up a spray can of WD-40. Well, WD-40 is excellent for rust and corrosion prevention on many things but it should never be used on lures. The smell and taste are completely foreign to fish. I explained all this to my host who in the next two hours spent washing every lure in the tackle boxes. My folly of enjoying all the pampering was not so enjoyable after all. In time my host became an accomplished angler and at the time of his death due to a heart attack, I rated him as an expert with lures. We had a lot of laughs over the lure-spraying incident.

In time all lures need some re-furbishing. Those used in salt water require it more often than those fished exclusively in fresh

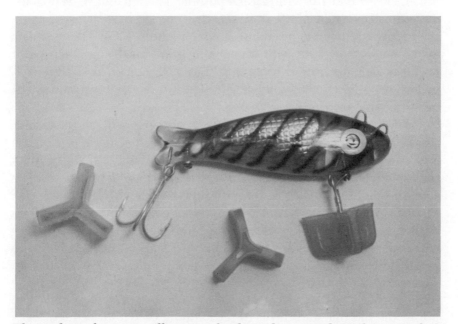

These plastic bonnets will protect hooks and prevent lures from tangling with other lures in tackle box.

water. This re-furbishing ranges from touching up the finishes and colors to replacing hooks and other metal components. Replacement hooks should be of the identical size as the originals. Replacements that are bigger or smaller can upset the balance of the lure and cause radical changes in its action. Once in a while the action change might be for the better, but usually the change decreases the lure's effectiveness.

In preparing material for this book I sent questionnaires to 25 lure manufacturers asking their views on the subject of changing hook sizes on lures. Twenty answered that such changes will seriously alter the action of surface and floating-diving plugs.

Lures moulded of plastic need no touch-up paint since the finishes are fused right into the product. Scratch marks from the teeth of big fish don't detract from effectiveness. If anything these scratches may help since they offer new surface angles to catch and reflect light.

Lures made of wood require considerable touch-up, for the finishes may start flaking off when scratches are made. Several companies offer lure touch-up kits so new scale finishes can be applied. The work is a bit messy and unless extra care is used, you are likely to end up with a disreputable looking finish. When my scale-finish wooden plugs start showing so much wear as to cause me to suspect they might be losing effectiveness, I solve the problem by buying a new lure with a spanking new finish and then paint over the beat up model to turn it into a standard red-white, red-yellow or yellow-white solid finish. These are the most consistent payoff colors anyway.

Metal spoons even with the best of care will show tarnish signs. This can be removed with silver polish. Out at sea or on the lake you can do a creditable tarnish-removing job by rubbing the spoon with wet tobacco. On the beachfront you can polish a spoon by lightly running it through fine, wet sand. Badly corroded spoons can be polished back to an effective shine by rubbing them with fine valve grinding compound. Some of the original plating will come off with the corrosion but this is unavoidable. This will mean additional polishing with the compound before each trip. This is a chore that can get old if you go fishing two or three times a week. An easy way out is to buy a new spoon, and then polish the old one and dip it in red, yellow or white lacquer. Even though the painted spoon may lack the flash of the metal finish, it will still get fish. The wobble of a spoon is deadly attractive to fish.

I owned one Johnson Sprite spoon that took fish under three flags so to speak. When I got the spoon about 12 years ago it was bright silver. Hard fishing in salt water took its toll and in time even polishing did little for it. So I dipped it in lacquer and turned it bright red . . . and caught a lot more fish. Then a few years back we had a tremendous king mackerel run in Galveston, Texas, offshore waters. When it came to casting spoons, it seemed the kings would only hit yellow. So I changed the spoon's flag to yellow . . . and it caught a lot of kings. Then one day as will happen in lure fishing, a big king broke my line and went swimming off into the sunset with my yellow spoon dangling from its lip. A lost lure but a happy memory. Oh well, all good things in life must eventually end.

17

FOR QUALITY FISHING

THERE is no such thing as only one "best" way to fish. Water and weather conditions and fish moods are too changeable for any single method to pay off best every time. Consequently the fisherman—whether he uses lures or natural baits—is faced with the "mood of the times" on every trip he makes. Lures may produce best one day, natural baits the next.

The artificial lure enjoys some decided advantages over natural bait and vice versa. Although the lure angler on many occasions will out-catch the fellow using natural bait, the average over the long run will show the natural bait fisherman as catching the most fish by far. So you might ask that if this is true, why use lures at all? Or why not just use lures when natural bait is not available? This is best answered by considering quality and quantity. The natural bait fisherman is going to end up with quantity, but he has little selectivity when it comes to quality. I don't mean he will not catch good fish, for he certainly will.

As an illustration let me point out what has happened to me on many occasions when using natural bait in both fresh and salt water. I have fished areas where I knew black bass to be, but the areas were also alive with bluegills and crappie. These little fellows have an insatiable appetite, and many times using natural baits I was never able to get to the blacks because the bluegills and crappie cleaned off the hook before the bass ever had a chance to move in. The same thing has happened in salt water fishing for speckled trout, redfish and pompano. Only in the case of salt water, the fish that kept cleaning off the hooks were piggies and catfish. Sure I caught plenty of bluegills, crappie, piggies and catfish, but I could have cared less for at the time I was seeking species other than these. I do not mind catching these little fellows for they can offer a lot of sport on light tackle. But when a fellow is seeking more regal species of fish, these little fellows become nothing more than annoying bait-stealers.

With natural bait a fisherman has no selectivity. He casts out and trusts to luck that some desirable species of fish will take the bait. He really never knows what will strike. If he likes this air of mystery, then fine and dandy. Otherwise natural bait fishing is pot luck fishing. I am not knocking it, because I do a lot of it.

The lure angler has a pretty good degree of selectivity in species. He uses baits that are proven fish-getters for certain species. He goes for black bass with lures that have the reputation for taking these fish. It is the same with other species of fish . . . in both fresh and salt water.

The lure fisherman has a decided advantage over the bait man when it comes to taking quality fish from an area with a heavy population of small panfish or bait-stealers. My experiences along this line are legion.

Remember the lure I referred to in the "I Fooled A Fish" chapter? Well, I bought that lure because of an earlier fishing trip experience. I was fishing natural bait—shrimp—for speckled trout in a shallow Texas bay, but all I was catching were hardhead catfish. Almost as soon as the bait hit the water on each cast, I would tangle with these bait-stealers. I probably never would have gotten the lure idea so early had not another wader passed by. He was casting a red and white sinking plug. On every fourth or fifth cast, he tied into a fish—not bait-stealing catfish like I was catching but nice fat speckled trout.

There was another occasion when I took out a visitor from Oklahoma City. I took along live shrimp for bait because the man confessed to never having fished salt water before. Live shrimp practically guarantee speckled trout if there are any around. But the visitor fooled me. He wanted to fish a spoon, so I let him try that while I stuck with the live shrimp. We both caught specks. I got one on almost every cast. He caught one on about every tenth cast. My fish were little stinkers barely over a pound each in size. The Oklahoman's fish ranged from four to seven pounds in weight. I caught the most fish on natural bait; the visitor caught the biggest —or quality—fish on lures. When I eventually put on a spoon, I started getting big ones, too. The lures gave us selectivity—and quality—rather than quantity.

If you fish to see how many fish you can catch on each trip, then by all means stick with natural baits. These are the baits that produce quantity.

Lures permit more accuracy in casting as well as more distance. The motion in casting a lure is smooth and graceful, and watching a good lure-caster in action is a symphony of movement. The fellow fishing natural bait is unable to use this same graceful poetry of motion. His cast is more of a chunk or swinging heave rather than a true cast. In lure-casting when the rod is started on the forward cast, it is done so with rapid force. The cast snaps the lure forward and propels it through the air like an arrow. Try this kind of casting with natural bait and you will snap the bait right off the hook. In casting out natural bait, the fisherman must start the forward cast gently and more swing or heave the bait out rather than shoot it out arrow-like. You just can't get much accuracy with a swing or heave, and you certainly will not be able to drop the bait within a three-foot circle at a distance of 60 or 70 feet with any consistency. But the lure angler has better control of his style of casting, and he can plunk the lure in the circle every time. And this is a presentation that pays off with fish.

The cast of the natural bait user is further impeded by a terminal rig that includes more than a baited hook. These extra—but necessary—things include sinkers, a second leader drop and bait, floats, etc. When all this stuff goes frailing through the sky, there is really little chance for any marked degree of accuracy. And all this stuff, too, offers wind resistance and cuts down on casting distance.

The artificial lure enables the angler to fish faster and cover much more territory than the fellow who uses natural baits. The time involved in re-baiting the hook is completely eliminated when lures are used. Then, of course, the problem of having to keep natural bait alive is completely eliminated.

18

THE RIGHT CONNECTIONS

THE connection of lure to leader is just like a marriage—or how well it lasts depends upon forethought and rationalization and not emotionalism. Fishermen are eternal optimists, and they invariably have visions of catching monster size fish. There is nothing wrong with a little dreaming. Just don't let those dreams lead to emotional mistakes. A mistake like using the wrong kind of leader—or spoiling lure action by connecting the lure to the leader with outlandish snap swivels, beaded chains, etc.

Modern lures, especially those turned out by reputable manufacturers, are rather delicately balanced little jewels. They may look like hunks of colored plastic with assortments of hooks and screw-eyes to some people, but they are far more than just that. Reputable manufacturers spend a lot of time and money with prototypes before they ever release the finished product to the public. True, the makers are out to catch the fisherman's money, but they will never get it unless their product also catches fish.

If the lure is supposed to be attached to the leader with a snap, it will either have a snap attached or the instruction sheet with the lure will advise use of a snap. Otherwise attach the lure directly to the leader with a knot, using either the blood or clinch knot and not the old-fashioned square knot. For the information of those unfamiliar with knots, the square knot has two distinct disadvantages. Number one, it is likely to slip under strain. Number two, the manner in which it "bites" into the line cuts the test strength of the line or leader by as much as 50 per cent. Hence a 10-pound test leader with a square knot will break at point of knot under a strain of about five pounds. Really it should be called the "robber" knot. The clinch or blood knot will reduce line test at point of knot, but only by approximately 10 per cent.

The fellow who uses monofilament line does not have to use

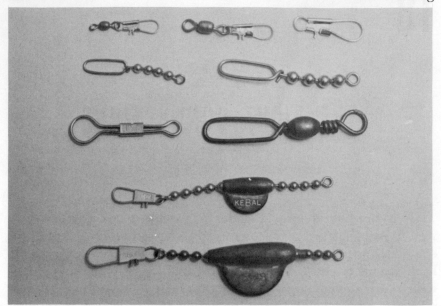

Types of hardware for attaching lures to leaders. Top to bottom: snaps with barrel swivels and plain snap; snaps on beaded chains; line connector and snap swivel; snaps on beaded chains with finned sinkers for trolling.

a separate leader. He can tie the lure directly to the line, just so long the line is not too heavy or bulky. With fish which have no teeth or only the faintest indication of teeth, there is absolutely no need for a wire leader. A wire leader will severely hamper lure action if the lure happens to be small in size.

Most top flight lure anglers shun snaps and snap-swivels like the plague. They use them only when absolutely necessary or when the original lure comes equipped with them. If a lure is designed to be fished without a snap or snap-swivel, the addiion of these items are likely to throw the lure off balance and detract from its fish-attracting ability.

There will be times when a wire leader must be used with a lure. This will be when you go after a fish with sharp teeth or troll in salt water. The proper way to troll-rig is to make a leader at least three feet long, using a barrel swivel at the end which attaches to the line and a snap or snap-swivel at the end which is attached to the lure. Twisting the wire directly to the screw-eye on the lure will hamper lure action seriously. Use of a snap or snap-swivel in this case will allow the lure to dangle freely. Almost all

Northern pike is one of several species of fresh-water fish that require use of wire leaders. Pike's mouth is all teeth.

lures sold for offshore trolling come equipped with snap or snap-swivel.

In heavy trolling use stainless steel wire. If you prefer casting instead of trolling, then go with supple braided wire that has a plastic coating. Use wire that complements the line. For example, if you are using 36-pound test line, it is ridiculous to use wire testing 200 pounds.

There are a few times when barrel swivels must be used in lure fishing. One is in the case of trolling for big gamefish. In this case the swivel is necessary since large fish when hooked often twist and spiral in the water. In a long fight such a fish can put a lot of twist in the line. The barrel swivel in this case should be used between line and leader. Another case for the swivel is with the lure that is designed to spin when retrieved. These lures, however, come equipped with swivel. If a second swivel is used with such a lure, it should be between leader and line and not between lure and leader.

The old salts say every little glitter counts when it comes to fishing lures. They are referring to the glitter on the lure itself . . . the metal lip, hooks, etc. They are not referring to stuff that glitters and sparkles three or four feet ahead of the lure. Hardware attachments between line and leader should be dull in color. Those stainless steel swivels look pretty, but they can result in a lot of lost fish and lures. It took some hard knocks experience to convince me of this years ago in Spanish mackerel and king mackerel fishing. I used to use bright swivels and many a time I had fish strike the flash of the swivel and cut the line. Now I use dull colored swivels, and if I can't find any, then I carefully paint black model airplane lacquer over the bright ones. Use care so as not to get any paint on the swivel's moving parts. This will cause them to stick and defeat the purpose of the swivel. There is one humorous incident connected with swivel painting. I had a whole box to paint one night, and when I tackled the job, my youngest daughter Laura June asked to help. I showed her how to do it and then gave her a brush. When I was not looking, she decided a faster way would be to dip the entire swivel into the lacquer bottle. I did not discover what had happened until the next day when I put the swivels to use in trolling for king mackerel.

There may be times when you will want to use a sinker ahead of the lure in order to fish deep. This is okay as long as the sinker is attached two to three feet ahead of the lure. Any sinker attached

Author with small barracuda, a salt-water species that requires both wire leader and swivel. These fish have habit of spinning in water and can put twist in line if no swivel is used.

Example of a combination artificial lure-natural bait rig for deep sea trolling. Small barracuda has tandem hooks sewed in its belly and an extra large feathered jig butted against its mouth, which is also sewed shut.

just a few inches . . . or even as much as a foot . . . ahead of the lure may hamper the lure's wiggling action.

Sinkers used in this connection should be either the trolling type or those with an eye at each end. The trolling sinker has a keel that prevents spinning. The clinch-on or dog-ear sinkers are poor choices as weights to be used with lures. The ears on these sinkers when bent over will often act like propellers and cause the entire sinker to spin. These sinkers are great for either putting a twist in the line or completely unraveling it.

If your lure has a swivel or there is the necessity of using a swivel between line and leader, check the swivel closely to make sure it is free of rust or corrosion and that it spins freely. A malfunctioning swivel only leads to trouble. I like to put a drop or two of fish oil on the moving parts of my swivels.

Check swivels frequently during the course of a fishing trip. They can pick up bits of marine vegetation and jam. This is more apt to happen in trolling than in conventional casting. The lure itself as well as its hooks should be checked for marine vegetation fouling. This fouling can spoil lure action. It is a good practice when trolling to every now and then reel in the line just to check the terminal hardware.

19

COMBINATION LURES

IF a fellow is going to be ultra successful in lure fishing, there will be times when he must do more than impart good action in the hardware.

Frequently fish will follow a lure right back to the boat but refuse to strike. Their attention has been captured but the lure apparently failed to fire up a mood for feeding . . . or one of anger or any of the other moods a fish might be capable of showing. It is most frustrating to see a fish follow a foot behind the lure, speed up when the retrieve is hastened, and stop when the retrieve is slowed down or stopped.

Many accomplished lure anglers get around this situation by improvising and using two lures, with one serving strictly as a teaser. It is quite like the offshore billfish fishermen who use a teaser to attract the big fellows in for a look-see at the baits trolled.

The teaser in lure fishing can be used in either plug or spoon fishing. The lure that the fish follow—but decline to hit—acts as the teaser. With a fine piece of monofilament line a second and much smaller lure is trailed behind the teaser. Usually this second lure is a fly, popping bug or small jig. Although the drag of this extra lure does cut down on the action of the teaser lure, it is not to such a degree as to cause the fish to quit following it.

Here is what happens in this kind of fishing. Invariably the fish will follow the big lure. Then when the fish sees the shadow of the boat or the fisherman, it will turn away, but in doing so it will almost always make some sort of pass at the trailing fly, bug or jig. This is the lure that catches the fish.

A second method of combination lures employing the trailer technique works well in fishing salt water bays. In this case a popping float is used three to four feet ahead of the lure which always is a sinking plug, lightweight spoon or jig. A popping float is one that has a concaved or dished top. When the line is retrieved,

Although wire leaders will hamper action of many lures, such leaders are necessary with fish having sharp teeth. Author's son Carl shows off Spanish mackerel's razor-like teeth.

the float leans over and creates a "gurgle" as it moves through the water. A sharp snap of the rod tip will cause the float to make a "plop" or "chug" sound. Either of these sounds is quite similar to the sound made when a fish hits a baitfish on top of the water.

The method of retrieve is one of moderate reeling, frequent pauses and occasional "chugs." The lure trailed beneath the float alternately swims, jumps and at times suspends motionless. This is quite an effective way to fish off-color water since sound is the principle means of initially catching the fish's attention. The clearer the water, the longer the leader necessary between lure and popping float. Difficulty in casting and water depth usually limit leader length to about five or six feet. In extremely clear water a lure rigged too close to the float is rather ineffective. I can only suppose that the size of the popping float might appear so foreign to the fish that it frightens it away. This perhaps may be the reason this sort of combination rig is used so seldom in fresh water, since fresh water is clear more often than salt water.

There is another combination that is quite deadly in trolling. This is the use of a spreader rig on which two lures—spoons, plugs, or jigs—are trolled side by side. The distance between the lures is usually about a foot. This is a deadly rig when it comes to working white bass when they school on the surface of a lake. It is also excellent for salt water trolling for fish up to about three or four pounds in size. It works for much larger fish, but one can have an awful lot of trouble trying to work in a pair of 15 or 20 pound king mackerel at the same time. A lot of good fishing rods have been broken this way.

Still another combination rig involves the use of live bait. It is a sort of half-lure, half-bait rig.

The most popular rig in salt water involves using double drop leaders. A hook with live bait is used on the top drop and a small spoon, plug or worm-jig is tied to the bottom drop. I have resorted to this rig on many occasions—occasions when fish would hit neither bait nor lure when fished alone. For some reason the fish would start striking when the bait-lure combination was used. Since fish have a sense of smell, perhaps the combination of smell with wiggling lure motion is what stirred them into action.

The same sort of rig is often used in fresh water fishing. Only in this case, the live bait is a minnow instead of a shrimp.

There is still another lure-bait combination that is most effective for black bass, northern pike, walleyes and lake trout. This is to put a strip of pork rind on the lure's back hook. That rind has a come-hither wave as interesting as a Hula girl's grass skirt. It can be fished effectively with either surface or sub-surface lures. A black pork rind is best for use with surface lures. Go to white rind when fishing sub-surface.

A fellow can get fine results down deep by using either a spoon

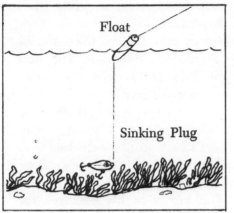

Fig. 1

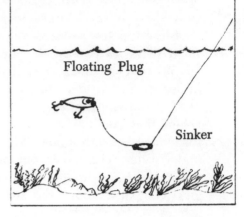

Fig. 2

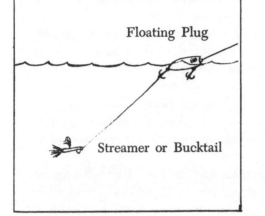

Fig. 3

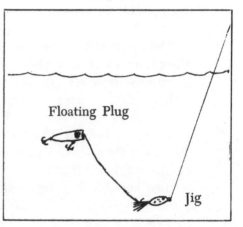

Fig. 4

Fig. 5

Fig. 6

or jig with pork rind. Again the best results come on white rinds since they are much easier to see than black.   ⊛

Either on the surface, sub-surface or down deep, the sense of smell plays no part in the lure-pork rind combination. The rind has no odor or smell. It is that tantilizing action with the come-hither wave that gives the fish interesting notions.

The drawings on page 133 show several popular and effective fish-getting combination lure rigs. Fig. 1 shows a sinking plug suspended beneath a float. Fig. 2 shows how to fish a floating lure under water. The sinker will carry the lure down. On the retrieve the sinker drags through the bottom vegetation while the lure wiggles along just above the snags. This rig is highly effective for fishing flooded stands of weeds.

The trailer rig is shown in Fig. 3. The teaser lure is a top water floater that "chugs" or "gurgles" on retrieve. The streamer fly or bucktail lure trails about 18 inches behind the floater.

Over a hard sand bottom free of snags, the combination in Fig. 4 is effective. The weighted jig will carry down the floating plug. On the retrieve the jig can be hippity-hopped along the bottom with the floating plug wiggling tantilizingly above it.

Fig. 5 shows how to work a long-lipped bottom-bumping plug over a sandy bottom. The lure is "walked" along the bottom so that the metal lip stirs up puffs of sand to give the impression of a small baitfish feeding on sand worms.

The lure-live bait rig is shown in Fig. 6. Live bait—shrimp or minnow—is rigged on a leader drop about 18 inches ahead of a lead-head jig, which is hippity-hopped along the bottom. This is a fine rig for catching two fish at the same time, especially if a fish hits the live bait first. The hooked fish in darting about will impart tantilizing action in the trailing jig, which is almost certain to be taken by another fish in the school.

20

A HARD NIGHT'S WORK

JAMES Heddon's plug and J. T. Buel's spoon were overnight productions. Modern day lures are produced even faster since they are either molded or stamped out by machinery. This, however, does not mean that a new lure is dreamed up one day and put on the market the next. How manufacturers wish the business was that simple!

Fishermen complain all the time about the cost of artificial lures. True, the materials used can be purchased for a few pennies. They don't take into account the machinery involved. Some of the high injection molding machinery can run into tens of thousands of dollars. And then even these machines don't turn out the finished product. There are many steps involved.

In the case of spoons it is stamping out, attaching hardware and packaging. The major steps in plug manufacture are molding, cementing, sanding, printing, assembling and packaging in that order. These are the big steps but within each major step there may be up to 12 additional operations. Jodie Grigg of Whopper Stopper, Inc., in Sherman, Texas, says: "Our most complicated lure pattern or finish is handled or goes through sixty-three (63) operations before it is boxed ready for shipment."

Whopper Stopper manufacturers Hellbender and Bayou Boogie lures, and each of these lures went through exhaustive research and development before they were ever put on the market. Grigg explains his company's operation like this:

"The development and testing of new lures usually requires from one to two years. Lures are designed to do a specific thing or perform a certain action. The all-purpose lure is a myth. If a plug is to be made of plastic, a model is usually constructed of wood. The wooden model is then tested for balance, action, etc. If correct, a plastic model is then made along the lines of the wooden model, carefully adding or removing plastic to duplicate

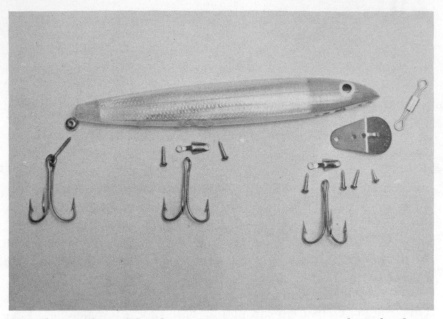

Note the number of hand operations necessary in attaching hardware to this Cisco Kid Musky plug. Labor represents major part in price of lures.

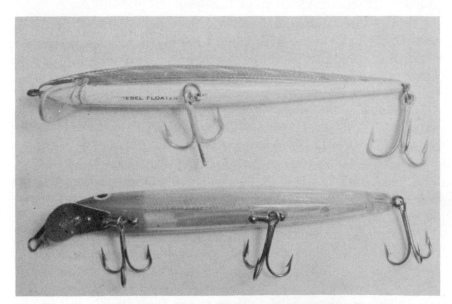

Attachment of hardware to Rebel Floater (top) requires less labor than attachments involved on Musky Cisco Kid (bottom).

the balance of the wooden model, and at the same time keeping simplicity of production in mind. Since most of the cost in manufacturing lures is in labor, this is vital to maintaining a popular list price. From the plastic model a temporary two-cavity mold is made to mold two halves or one complete lure per shot. Samples are then sent to our sales representatives for testing either by them or by good fishermen in their territory. While this is going on, the lure is being thoroughly tested at the factory. Reports are then sent in as to action, fishability, performance, productivity and suggested changes, if any. If changes are made, we go through the procedure again. If no changes are made, permanent tooling is made and the new lure introduced on August 1st to the trade for next year."

Dick Kotis of the Fred Arbogast Co., of Akron, Ohio, reports his company tests prototypes two to three years before going into production for the market.

Cotton Cordell of Cordell Fishing Tackle of Hot Springs, Arkansas, says approximately a year goes into testing each model produced by his company.

Anyone who thinks lure testing is nothing more than casting in a swimming pool is dead wrong. A certain amount of testing is done in pools, but it is to see how the lure acts under various retrieve speeds, with various types of leader material and a variety of hardware attached. When the manufacturer gets the exact action he desires, the tests move to waters inhabited by fish. Then under all conditions—clear, sandy, calm, and rough water—the lure is given a thorough workout to determine its ability as a fish-getter. Lure manufacturers know full well there are times when fish will hit anything that plunks into the water, but they are not going to base their advertising claims on such conditions. Consequently lures are field tested day after day for months and not just a few weeks.

Many a would-be lure maker has carved out a product, put it on the market without exhaustive field tests and ended up losing his shirt. Without using any names, let me cite the case of one man.

He was a tackle tinkerer—and there is nothing wrong in that. We need such people who are willing to experiment, for without them the world would stand still. This fellow carved a plug out of wood. He fished it and had good results on a number of occasions under various water and weather conditions. He had visions of making a fortune. He invested in equipment to mold plastic duplicates of the wooden model. He turned out a great number of plastic lures. In his rush for the pot of gold, he had either forgotten to or skipped over making a plastic copy and testing it. His lure hit the market advertised as a "floater-diver" plug. The specific gravity of wood and plastic are rather far apart, and in short order tackle stores and fishermen started bombarding him with complaints that "the damned thing doesn't float but sinks like a rock." The action obtained with the wooden prototype was a far cry from that of the plastic copies. I have never been able to verify it, but I heard that his little venture cost him something like $20,000.

And it all happened because he did not take the time to thoroughly field test the lure. Lure makers today are as finicky over their products as a mother is over her daughter's wedding dress.

Reputable and established lure manufacturers are not going to put duds on the market. If you follow the instructions that come with a lure and give it a fair trial, it will catch fish. And by fair trial I don't mean a dozen casts or a single fishing trip. After all you must remember there will be days when a fellow can't even get a strike on natural bait.

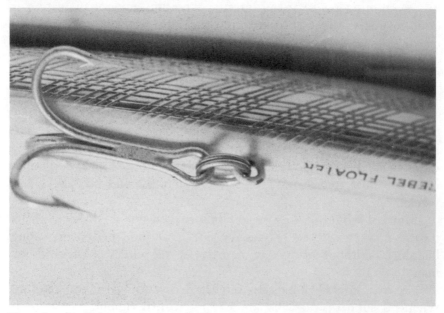

How hooks hang from lure belly can have effect on overall action. Treble hook should be attached so that when lure moves through water, two tines will straddle body. With just one hook tine down, lure is less likely to snag up on brush. In retrieve this Rebel Floater plug would be moving through water from left to right.

When a lure gets a reputation as a fish-taker, it can grow into a giant in the fishing field, and it can mushroom a small business into one of national scope.

Consider the story of the PICO Perch manufactured by the Padre Island Co. of San Antonio, Texas.

Back in 1933 a World War I veteran started carving small replicas of baitfish found in Texas coastal waters. His wood carvings were of a baitfish, colloquially called the piggy perch, a common pigfish and a member of the grunt family. The wooden piggy perch armed with hooks caught salt water fish and fresh water fish. Originally manufactured in Corpus Christi, Texas, the lure was called the PICO Perch, getting its name from the initials of the company, the Padre Island Co.

Pico switched to plastic shortly after World War II, and the company began to develop new colors and sizes. The popularity of the lure stems from the fact that it swims like a fish and is difficult to retrieve incorrectly. The lure enjoyed its initial popularity in Texas—and then the entire Southwest. Today it is known and used in every state in the Union, Canada, Mexico, and South America. It is a lure designed for salt water fishing, but one that has proven to be just as effective in fresh water.

If you purchase a lure for $1.50 in a retail tackle store, you enrich the manufacturer by approximately 68 cents. So if a lure company sells 100,000 lures annually, the manufacturer pockets $68,000. Oh, if this was only true!

The lure goes from manufacturer to factory representative to wholesale distributor and then to retail outlet. Each hand gets a piece of the action. The wholesale distributor pays approximately 68 cents per lure on $1.50 retail models. This distributor in turn adds a healthy commission when he sells to the retail outlet, which again adds to the price bringing it up to $1.50.

Out of the 68 cents the manufacturer gets such items as federal excise tax (10 per cent), sales commission to factory representative, freight, packaging, advertising, cataloguing and literature eat up approximately 32 cents. This leaves the manufacturer with 36 cents. But this is not net profit. The manufacturer still has his overhead of material, labor, insurance, utilities and more taxes to pay. He usually ends up with a net profit of about 10 cents a lure. Obviously he must sell a tremendous number of lures to make a living.

So getting back to the annual sales of 100,000 lures carrying a retail price of $1.50 each, the manufacturer ends up with a net profit ranging from $10,000 to $15,000, depending on how well he manages his operation to cut costs.

The manufacturer can make a larger net profit per lure by selling mail order direct to the customer, but past experiences have proven that this is not economically feasible because of limited product exposure. Remember not every fisherman who walks into the retail tackle store reads the magazine in which the lure manufacturer advertises. In the long run the manufacturer does better by taking a smaller profit per lure by letting the distributors and retailers do the marketing.

Even with such a small net profit per lure to the manufacturer, lures obviously sell well, otherwise the makers would not stay in business.

There is no way of getting figures on the total number of lures sold annually unless one could get Internal Revenue Service figures and feed them into a computor. These figures, of course, are unobtainable since they are confidential information between the various manufacturers and the IRS.

In 1967 there were 27,000,000 fishing licenses sold in the United States. It is estimated that another 10,000,000 through resident or age exemptions or just plain violating the law fished without licenses. How many of these fishermen used lures?

Again there are no figures available and I will have to go on estimates supplied from questionnaires sent to a number of lure makers. The manufacturers themselves estimated the number of regular lure fishermen runs 15 to 18 percent of the total number of fishermen. Based on the 27,000,000 licensed fishermen this would range from 4,050,000 to 4,860,000 lure anglers. According to answers on the questionnaires, manufacturers indicated the average lure fisherman buys two dozen lures a year. Using the 15 per cent figure (4,050,000) of 27,000,000, this would bring the total number of lures sold in 1967 to 97,200,000. This is only for the United States. Remember that many lures made in this country are worldwide in distribution.

If the 97,200,000 figure sounds hard to believe, let me use some actual figures on a home operation that involves my entire family. Strictly on a spare time basis we make wire fishing leaders for a wholesale distributor. In a 12-month period we made 30,000 and the wholesaler sold them all in Galveston, Texas, County alone. And on top of that the wholesaler said recently he hoped we could increase our production the following year. The leader we make is one of nine types this wholesaler distributes. He told me that in round numbers he moves a quarter of a million leaders a year, and again all of them just in Galveston County.

Wholesale fishing tackle distributors with whom I checked seem to feel that lure manufacturers are low in their percentage estimates. Most felt the percentages (15 to 18) were about right for fresh water fishing but were far low in regards to salt water fishing. They scaled the percentages on salt water lure users from 20 to as high as 35 per cent.

One tackle representative whose territory covers four states said this:

"Ninety per cent of the fishermen I run into have lures in their tackle boxes. All of them don't use them. Some have lures for show purposes only, and I guess they figure if someone sees them with lures, then that person will tag them as real fishermen. I guess you might call it a sort of status symbol among some fishermen. I would say half of that 90 per cent uses lures occasionally, with 25 to 30 per cent of the 90 per cent using them exclusively. If lures didn't sell good, you wouldn't hear live bait dealers cuss them so much."

The lure industry has grown so to speak from an acorn into a mighty oak, and it is here to stay.

The first Heddon catalog in 1902 listed a single lure, the Dowagiac floater. A year later, Heddon's catalog listed two lures, the original floater and a sinking model. When the company put out its 1910 publication, it listed a third type of lure, this being the floater that ran underwater on retrieve. At the 1968 American Fishing Tackle Manufacturers Association tackle showing in Chicago, Heddon listed a total of 691 different lures for every type of fishing.

In 1968 there were approximately 200 lure manufacturing companies in the United States. These were companies that operated full time. Tackle representatives tell me that when "garage" operations and spare time makers are taken into consideration, the figure runs into the thousands.

21

DO IT YOURSELF

AT some time in the life of every lure fisherman, the fellow will be haunted by the ghosts of James Heddon and J. T. Buel. By this I mean the man gets the urge to build a "better mouse trap." The pioneer spirit—perhaps with visions of the million dollar idea— comes to the front, and the fellow hauls out his tools and gets down to the business of producing a lure all of his own. Actually this is how many very popular lures today got their start.

Do-it-yourself luring is a lot of fun. You will produce some that are effective fish-getters; others that will be real duds. If you produce a really new successful lure, chances are you will be able to sell the idea to an established lure manufacturer and make a few bucks. Truthfully, however, I would not count on becoming a millionaire.

By far the easiest way to make your own lures is to buy a kit. These kits, which are offered by a number of companies, contain instructions and all the necessary material. You can follow the instructions and produce a model that has already been proven to be a fish-getter. Or you can throw the instructions away and boldly turn the materials into a creation of your own imagination. There are kits on the market today for plugs, spoons, jigs and flies. You name it and somebody has it.

But let's assume you have more pioneering blood in your veins and you want to make a lure from scratch. Although your wife may not approve, the kitchen tableware is a good starter if you have spoons in mind. You can use teaspoons, tablespoons and even big kettle spoons. Tricky action elongated spoons can be fashioned from the handles of spoons or the handles of forks. I know a couple of fellows who made some pretty good spoons out of the blades of butter knives.

When it comes to plugs, you can use plastic or wood for the bodies. I have seen the plastic handles of knives, toothbrushes, etc., carved into working lures. These, of course, are all sinking or under

Kits containing full instructions and material for making several dozen lures can be purchased for less than $10. (Courtesy The Worth Company)

water lures, since the specific gravity of solid plastic is such that it will not float.

If you want a floating plug, you will have to go to wood. Balsa wood is excellent for top water baits. It is easy to carve and light enough to float high in the water even when hardware is attached. Balsa plugs, however, have two drawbacks. First, these lures are very light and can be rather difficult to cast, especially into the wind. Next the wood is soft, and if fish with sharp teeth are involved, you can expect the lure to take a hell of a beating. I have had some of my balsa wood creations shredded to splinters by king mackerel, barracuda and dolphin. Sort of like that alligator gar did to my little red and white model boat years ago. But even when you make a lure that is ripped to pieces by fish, you get the satisfaction of feeling you really fooled a fish.

Cedar is excellent for lure bodies, and it can be carved into surface plugs, although it will not float nearly so high in the water as balsa. Its big advantage over balsa is that it is hard and will take a beating without showing serious battle wounds. With the addition of a metal lip, this plug can be turned into a floater-diver. Metal lips can be purchased or they can be robbed from old lures that may be beyond repair.

The cedar plug can be turned into a sinking or strictly under-water lure by the addition of lead weight within the lure body. Location of the lead will determine the action. The closer the lead is placed to the front of the lure, the more pronounced the lure's wiggle. If the weight is located just slightly forward of center, the lure action will be one of slow but wide-sweeping wiggles. Weight located near the rear end of the plug will cause it to travel through the water with little or no wiggle.

The lead can be placed in the plug by drilling a hole com-pletely through the wood. Then melt some lead and pour it into the hole and allow it to harden. This can badly scorch and even set balsa wood on fire. With cedar, however, there will be only a slight scorch mark, which will be sanded away and painted over anyway. Either file or sand the lead dowel flush with the lure body. A word of caution about the location of the lead insert. I mentioned how its location will determine lure wiggle. Well, make sure the lead is inserted in the lower part of the lure's body. If it is placed above the centerline, the lure will turn upside down in the water.

Model airplane lacquers are the best for lure finishes. They come in a great variety of colors, dry quickly and have a shine that flashes. To seal the wood against moisture absorption, use several coats. My method is to completely dip a plug in a can of lacquer. After it dries, then I dip it in a second time. I always use white as the base color. The other colors can be painted on by hand, or you can put masking tape on the plug and spray on the lacquer. Personally I don't think it makes a lot of difference if the various lines are exactly straight or wavy. After all when a plug is wiggling through the water, I doubt if a fish really takes the time—or has the reasoning power—to be concerned about straight or wavy lines.

If you don't want to go to the expense of purchasing a mold to cast jigs, you can get the job done adequately with sinkers. The clinch-on or dog-ear sinkers and the oblongs with a metal ring at each end are excellent for making jigs.

With clinch-on or dog-ear sinkers you must use a single hook with a long shank. Pry the opening slit that runs the length of the sinker wide enough so that the hook shank can be laid in it. Crimp the sinker slit shut and bend over the dog-ears to hold the hook

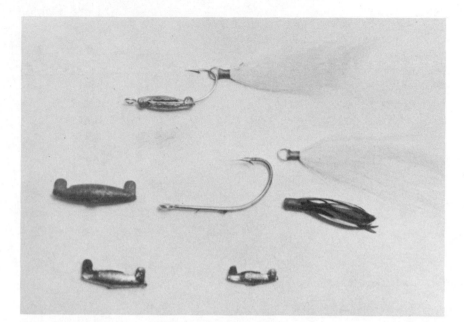

With hooks, pinch-on sinkers, bucktails, and rubber skirt, do-it-yourself jigs can be made on the spot.

firmly in place. Again model airplane lacquer can be used for whatever finish you desire. You can dress it up more by adding a bucktail on the hook.

Treble or gang hooks can be used with the ringed oblong sinkers. Attach the hook to one eye of the sinker with a small split ring. At the same time you might desire to add a bucktail. Finish off the lead portion of this jig with lacquer. You can make a rather long jig with this sinker by attaching the hook to it with a line connector instead of a split ring. If you do this, you must add a bucktail to the hook, for when fishing the hook will be riding as much as an inch—maybe even more depending upon the size connector used—behind the painted body. You don't want the fish striking at the body only. Consequently the addition of a bucktail on the hook will help to direct the fish's attention to the business end.

Objects that can be turned into do-it-yourself lures are legion. To mention just a few, I have made and caught fish on lures made out of ball point pens, plastic butts off cigars, metal rings and tabs from pop-top cans, bunches of rubber bands knotted together at one end and strips of aluminum foil. All caught fish.

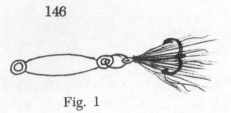

Fig. 1

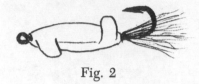

Fig. 2

Fig. 3

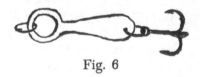

Fig. 4

Fig. 5

Fig. 6

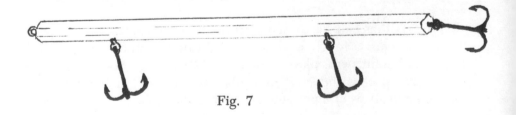

Fig. 7

Personally I prefer to go with manufactured lures, but every now and then I still like to turn out something of my own creation. I imagine it is a manner of satisfying my ego in proving to myself that I really am smarter than a fish. "I fooled a fish" is really a great feeling, something akin to kissing a girl for the first time.

The sketches on page 146 show several easy to make do-it-your-self lures. In Fig. 1 a treble hook with bucktail is attached with split ring to a ringed sinker. In Fig. 2 a long shanked hook with bucktail is inserted in the split of a dog ear sinker. The hook is held in place by crimping over the dog ears.

A batch of rubber bands is bound securely just behind the eye on a long shank hook in Fig. 3. Fig. 4 shows a discarded plastic mouthpiece from a cigar fashioned into a surface popper with the insertion of a balsa wood dowel and addition of a treble hook. In Fig. 5 the lure is the same as in Fig. 1, only with aluminum foil wrapped around the sinker. The foil is shredded at the end so it will flutter around the tines of the hook. Fig. 6 shows a metal can ring-top turned into a lure by the addition of a split ring up front and a split ring and treble hook at the rear. In Fig. 7 a ball point pen hull is made into an underwater "stick" lure by addition of a screw-eye at the front and three sets of treble hooks.

22

CATCHY NAMES

IF all the lures ever made were catalogued under one cover, the publication would be equal in size to the telephone directory of a large size city. Under each "family name" (manufacturing company) would be listed dozens of offspring (individual lure) names. It is interesting to note that the offspring names are those that the fishermen remember. When it comes to remembering manufacturers' names, they are not worth a darn.

To illustrate this point let me list 15 nationally known lures. Then test yourself to see if you can come up with the names of the manufacturing companies. The lures include: (1) Hawaiian Wiggler, (2) Jitterbug, (3) Hellbender, (4) Bayou Boogie, (5) River Runt, (6) Lucky 13, (7) Jointed-Pikie, (8) Reb 2, (9) Daredevle, (10) Hot Spot, (11) Thin Fin, (12) Shimmy Gal, (13) Bass-Oreno, (14) Kastmaster and (15) Flatfish.

Twelve different companies are represented by the 15 lures. Lure Nos. 1 and 2 are made by the Fred Arbogast Co. Whopper Stopper Inc., makes Nos. 3 and 4. Heddon manufactures Nos. 5 and 6. The other manufacturers represented are (7) Creek Chub Bait Co., (8) Norman Manufacturing Co. Inc., (9) Lou J. Eppinger Co., (10) Cordell Fishing Tackle Co., (11) Storm Manufacturing Co., (12) Creme Lure Co., (13) South Bend Bait Co., (14) Acme Tackle Co., and (15) Charles Helin Tackle Co.

Given names for lures like given names for humans are easiest to remember. Surnames just seem to throw people. It is far easier for a fisherman to go into a tackle store and ask for a River Runt than it is to ask for a Heddon No. 340, even though they are one and the same. Zip codes, area codes, service serial numbers, and social security numbers are tough enough without foisting a numbering system on fishermen.

Within the trade, however, all manufacturers identify lure models by code numbers. It takes a store buyer a lot less time to fill out a Heddon order form for ten 340 models than it does to write out "River Runt." To further simplify matters in ordering, color finishes are coded by numbers, letters or a combination of both. For example, a buyer's order to Heddon for ten 340JRH simply means he wants ten River Runts in the frog scale, red head finish. The JRH is Heddon's code for frog finish red head.

Lure manufacturers seek catchy names for their products and names that are easy to remember. They also know that many outdoor writers in their daily fishing reports for their papers list what lures the fishermen use. A catch listed on a "frog finish red head River Runt" means more to other fishermen than does 340JRH. Typographical errors will crop up and if the 340JRH comes out 320JRH, the lure will be a Tiny Crazy Crawler, which in addition to being fished in a different manner has a different action than a River Runt.

Lure names are arrived at in many different ways. Consider the Daredevle spoon. Its maker Lou J. Eppinger got the name from the U.S. Marines who were nicknamed "Daredevils" in World War I. But Eppinger had some concern about how the public would accept "devil." So when he named his spoon, he purposely misspelled the word to come out "devle." Whether its "devil or "devle" Lou's spoon will be around for a long time because it is an excellent fish-getter.

The Doug English Lure Co. came up with a winner when Doug English decided to name one of his lures "Bingo." He stumbled on the name while the lure was still in field testing stages. He caught fish after fish on it, and then after one catch he exclaimed: "Bingo, another fish!" And so the name stuck. This lure is now put out in four sizes and graduating from the smallest to the largest are named Bingo, Queen Bingo, King Bingo, and Super Bingo. It is a catchy name for a fish-catching lure.

Unfortunately it takes more than a catchy name for a lure to take fish. Consequently some catchy-named lures have died on the vine. I won't use any of the died-on-the-vine names for obvious reasons.

Let's go on to the names of some successful lures. Some give a hint as to the action of the lure. For example, Heddon puts out a rapidly vibrating plug that attracts fish on the principle of sound. Appropriately it is called the Sonic. Then there is the Dying Flutter, a name that indicates the lure has the action of a dying and fluttering minnow. Charles Helin's Flatfish is shaped like a small flatfish.

Pico's Piggy Perch is named after the piggy perch that is a popular baitfish on the Gulf Coast.

One of Fred Arbogast's earliest lures was the Hawaiian Wiggler. The name fit to a T because the lure had a rubber skirt that wiggled like the grass one worn by a Hawaiian hula dancer. Arbogast also put out a lure called the Hula Dancer. Both the Wiggler and Dancer are real fish-getters.

To the uninitiated, mention of a Devil Horse or Devil Warhorse conjurs up visions of some sort of fiery horse. To the fisherman it is not a horse at all, but a darned good stick lure for fresh water fishing. Sometimes a move is made to capitalize on a popular trend of the times. The Heddon Tiger and Wood's Dipsy Doodle are good examples. The Dipsy Doodle came out just about the time when the song "The Dipsy Doodle" was popular. Heddon's Tiger came out right after the Humble Oil and Refining Company popularized its sales slogan of "Put a Tiger in your tank." The 1968 Heddon catalogue boldly heads the page illustrating its Tiger lures with "Put a Tiger in your tackle box."

Catchy names for lures are legion and here are just a few of some fine fish-getters: Bomber, Bushwacker, Whopper Stopper, Hellbender, Bayou Boogie, Spook, Zara, Punkinseed, Commando, Hootie, Bass-Grabber, Mr. Champ, Hot Spot, Gay Blade, Lucky 13, Shyster, Knucklehead and No Alibi.

I recall the days when a Ford was a Ford, a Plymouth a Plymouth and an Oldsmobile an Oldsmobile. We still have the same car manufacturers around but they hang names like Mustang, Fairlane, Barracuda, Cutlass, etc., on their products. Catchy names seem to have some magical selling power. It seems that in the lure business catchy names catch fishermen. If the lures then catch fish, then the manufacturer has a winner.

Until the advent of spinning tackle in this country, lures were made in rather uniform weights and sizes. For general baitcasting the weights used to run around ⅝th of an ounce for fresh water and a half-ounce for salt water. There were, of course, heavier lures for open lake and high seas fishing. Spinning gear brought upon the scene much lighter lures, including some down to 1/16th of an ounce in weight. This in turn led to the production of small versions of already highly successful lures that formerly could be handled only on baitcasting tackle. Consequently we now have companies producing the same lure ranging from midget models of ⅛th of an ounce on up to three and four ounces. For example,

Whopper Stopper's popular Bayou Boogie weights ⅝th of an ounce. The company has a giant size for salt water fishing and this model weighs three ounces.

The weight and size range in spoons is even greater. Acme Tackle Co. manufactures the same model Kastmaster spoon in eight sizes scaling upward from ⅛th of an ounce to three ounces.

23

GETTING UNSNAGGED

EVEN though I have a great number of lures in my tackle boxes, I still dislike losing any to snags. And I say this in view of the fact that most of the lures were given to me as samples. If I have to part with a lure, I prefer it to happen in one of two ways. One is to have a big fish take it away, because this is a thrill in itself. The other is to give the lure to someone who can make use of it. In fact, I have started a number of fellows in lure fishing in just this manner. A number of lure makers know this and this is probably the reason they periodically send me samples.

The loss of a lure by a fellow who has to purchase each and every one is not so easy to take. And when you get down into some of the flooded timber bottoms in the South, lure losing can get quite expensive.

There are ways to get lures unsnagged and these ways are up for discussion in this chapter.

For a starter a fellow can purchase any of a number of devices marketed as lure retrievers. Most are usually nothing more than miniature weighted grappling hooks. You let them slide down your line via a large split-ring or clip. The device, of course, has a very stout line attached. When the device hits the snagged lure, the theory is that its weight will knock the lure free. It does not always happen this way and often quite a lot of vigorous jigging is needed. Even then lures are not always knocked free. Still the devices are worth the money because they will free most of the normal snags.

You can make your own lure-freer by screwing a number of screws part-way into a six-ounce sinker, which is attached to the fishing line by means of a clip or line connector.

The surest lure-freer I have run across yet is one that I made from an old cane pole. The pole is about 12 feet long. I have mounted on the tip end a large rod tip top, with a large line connector attached to one side. When I get a snag, I open the line

Illustrated are a few types of weed guards. Lure at left has twin guards that ride open. Guards on other two lures lock in place under tension. The guards release and spring open exposing the hook point when fish bites down on lure.

connector and slip the fishing line into it. The connector is then closed so that the line will not slip out. This connector will keep the tip of the cane pole alongside the line and lure as I probe the depths. When the cane pole tip comes in contact with the snagged lure, I do a lot of jabbing and twisting. The pole gives me leverage with which to work, and in digging lures out of bad snags, this is most important.

If the water in which I am fishing is less than six feet deep, I free snagged lures simply by sticking my rod down into the water and reeling until the tip top hits the lure. Then a little jabbing and twisting will usually do the job. Actually a lot of hard jabbing is not necessary if you use a system in unsnagging lures. Whenever I snag up, my first efforts to free the lure are a few twitches of the rod tip. If this does not work, then I allow slack in the line, for sometimes the lure will fall free of its own accord. If this fails, then I move right over the lure and start probing with the cane pole if the water is deep or with the rod tip if the water is shallow.

Most fishermen make the mistake of trying to free lures by

tugging them loose. All they succeed in doing is to bed the hooks deeper and deeper into the tree stump, log or what have you.

If you have no lure retriever or cane pole and the water is too deep for rod tip probing, you can try freeing the lure by paddling the boat to the opposite side of the snag. This works well when lures foul between or under rocks, since the hooks won't dig in to anything. It is successful to a lesser degree when logs and stumps are involved, because in these cases the hooks are usually dug into something well past the barb.

There are three other methods I have found successful in unsnagging lures. These involve the line and the hooks on the lures.

If the fish I am after do not have hard mouths, I change hooks on the lures and put on types that will bend or straighten out under sustained tension. I make sure the hooks are the same size as those replaced so there is no change in the weight to upset the balance or action of the lure. The first time a fishing companion saw me make these hook changes and heard my reasons, he showed con-

In fishing rocky waters, weed guards can be left open as illustrated on these jig-worms. Springiness of guards will cause lures to bounce off rocks. In waters where hooks are likely to bed into soft objects, guards should be locked in place.

siderable alarm and exclaimed: "But you're going to lose fish when
they straighten out the hooks too!"

This would be so if hard-mouthed fish are involved, but with
soft-mouthed fish there is little problem in holding a 25 pound fish
with a hook that will straighten out under 15 pounds sustained
strain. This is easy to understand when you remember that in snagging up, the strain on the hook is at the point of the hook. When
the same hook penetrates through the flesh of a soft-mouthed fish,
the strain is not at the point but at the *bend* of the hook. It takes
a lot more strain to straighten out a hook at this spot. When hard-
mouthed fish are involved, the hook is likely to penetrate only a
little past the barb. Consequently the strain is put near the point
and the hook will straighten out rather easily. If this same hook
penetrates to its bend, it will hold a rather large hard-mouthed fish.

There is one important thing you must do after you free lures
by straightening out hooks. First the hook must be rebent to shape
with pliers, but after this is done a half dozen times, the hook will
be weakened considerably and will break because of metal fatigue.
After three or four straightenings and rebendings, I simply replace
the hook with a new one. I would rather throw away a five cent
hook than lose a good fish because of a hook with metal fatigue.

This Du-Dad plug is a surface noise-maker with weed guards atop its
back. This plug can be fished across floating weed beds and lily pads
without snagging up.

I do a lot of fresh water fishing in East Texas ponds, oxbow lakes and rivers. Some are nightmares of snags, particularly when it comes to casting lures near the shorelines or into pockets where there is a lot of overhanging trees and brush. I could free my lures by paddling the boat right into the stuff, but I have had too many close encounters with water moccasions. I don't enjoy having them drop off tree limbs and right into the boat.

So when I fish these spots, I go with reels filled with heavy test monofilament line—line testing about 40 pounds. With ⅜th and half-ounce lures there is relatively little trouble in casting with such heavy line, unless extremely long casts are involved. But fortunately in heavy brush there is little need for long casts. When I snag up in this kind of brush, the lure usually can be freed by simply straining on the 40-pound test line. I may pull up all kinds of logs off the bottom, but it beats going back into the dark, dank overhanging limbs and risking an angry cottonmouth moccasin in the boat.

The subject of snakes brings up another matter in lure fishing. Unless you fish in Alaska or Hawaii, you will do almost all of your fresh water fishing in waters inhabited by poisonous snakes. At some time or other you will have snakes swim by within casting distance. Resist the urge to scare off the snake by plunking the lure into the water near it. I did it once, dropping the lure in the water about six feet ahead of the snake. The snake immediately went under, I thought I had frightened it off—and then a second or so later I had a tremendous strike. That old snake—one of the meanest looking cottonmouths I have ever seen—struck the lure and got a mouthful of hooks. I did not reel in a single foot of line. I just cut it and let the snake swim off, violently shaking its head to get rid of my Lucky 13 plug. Now when I fish snake infested waters, I carry along a few rocks. I chase away swimming snakes by throwing rocks rather than lures. It is just as effective and 100 per cent cheaper.

I lost one other lure to a snake. It was in a flooded stand of cypress trees in Louisiana. Black bass were working well but they were all laying close to the tree trunks and cypress knees. To get them one had to work floating plugs within a foot or so of these hideouts. I was fishing a frog-finish Jitterburg at the time. I had the plug "gurgling" within a foot of a cypress knee not more than 20 feet from the boat. Wham! A big rattlesnake struck right off the top of the cypress knee and hooked himself well. I never did see the snake before it struck. This was another time when I just cut the line and paddled out to a bit more open water.

24

SOME DO, SOME DON'T

ALL types of lures will catch fish but all species of fish won't hit lures. Some fish readily take one type of lure but strike only occasionally at other types. There are also a few species that are quite cosmopolitan and will take all types of artificial lures.

The fresh water black bass is the most cosmopolitan of the lot. Regardless of what name this fish is known by—largemouth, bronzeback, green trout, to mention a few—the black bass is a fish that will strike anything you might happen to have in the tackle box. This fish will take strictly surface lures, floaterdivers, deep runners and bottom bumpers. It will strike big lures as well as small ones. It will take plugs, spoons, jigs, plastic worms and flies. Its willingness to strike every type of lure plays a major role in making it America's No. One fresh water gamefish.

Smallmouth bass are nearly as willing as their bigger cousins to go for artificial lures, although they are less likely to go for strictly surface plugs.

Some fresh water species show discrimination when it comes to lure size. The muskellunge, northern pike, walleye and lake trout are good examples. Although these fish are occasionally caught on small lures, the use of large lures will get a fellow a lot more action. Every guide I have fished with in Canadian waters has always advised using big lures—brutish lures ranging six to eight inches in length. In spite of the fact that there are times when muskies and northerns hit surface lures, these fish show a decided preference for hardware that runs a few feet below the surface. Northerns can be caught consistently on top water plugs only when the fish school up in shallow water with grass stands.

Lake trout very rarely hit surface lures. The big trophy size fish are invariably caught deep and usually by trolling the lure 40 to 60 feet down. When a lure runs this deep, it must be large and flashy in order to be seen, and this dictates that spoons are the main choice. Schoolsize lakers, however, can be taken in considerably shallower water and especially when the water temperature ranges from around 39 to 45 degrees. Within this temperature range school lakers—fish five to 10 pounds in size—like to move into water around 20 feet deep and especially to areas where swiftly flowing river waters discharge into lakes.

This angler has a string of America's fresh water favorite, the black bass. Much of this fish's popularity stems from its willingness to hit all kinds of lures with all kinds of actions. (Louisiana Tourist Commission photo)

But even in relatively shallow water, lake trout like big lures. I have caught these fish measuring 24 to 32 inches in length in Canadian Northwest Territories lakes on spoons and plugs measuring six inches long. I have had occasions when these fish hit big spoons and plugs but completely shunned identical plugs and spoons only three inches long.

Texas fisherman R. D. King with a black crappie. This fish is particularly fond of striking at small spinners.

Texan Dave Taylor with a pair of speckled trout, a fish also known as the spotted sea trout. These fish will strike a wide variety of artificial lures. (Galveston Beach Park Board Photo)

Redfish, or channel bass as they are known on the Atlantic Coast, are caught frequently on lures in some waters but are most obstinate about lures in other waters. For example, big redfish are often taken on artificial lures on the Atlantic Coast. Throw the same lures at big redfish in the Texas and Louisiana surf and you will wear out your arm casting. In these waters one has to use natural baits to catch big redfish consistently. Perhaps water temperature and clarity, bottom composition and degree of bottom slope or dropoff has something to do with this. Atlantic Coastal waters are generally clearer and cooler than those found along Texas and Louisiana. Water depth along the Texas and Louisiana coasts increases gradually, while depths along the Atlantic Coast sheer off and increase quite rapidly.

Big sailfish such as this are occasionally caught on artificial lures. Anglers after sailfish will have better luck fishing with natural baits. (Courtesy The Galveston Daily News)

Salt water fish are much more hesitant about hitting surface lures than are their fresh water cousins. The man who wants top water lure action with any degree of consistency must do his fishing in shallow bay flats or at night. In shallow salt water bay fishing, most gamefish show a decided preference for medium size spoons and jigs.

Fish like Spanish mackerel, king mackerel, cobia, dolphin and bonita are migratory fish and are often called "surface feeders." They feed near the surface, but in the true sense of surface feeding they rarely take their food right off the surface. I have caught these species on strictly surface plugs but the occasions have been quite rare. These fish show a preference for lures worked a few feet below the surface. You can troll two identical lures through a school of king mackerel and mop up on kings with the lure riding three or four feet down but get absolutely nothing on the lure running 20 feet deep.

Salt water fishermen who go for flounders or gafftopsail catfish will find themselves wasting time trying to catch these fish on artificial lures. Although both species have been caught on artificials, they show a decided preference for natural baits. At certain times of the year, however, flounders can be taken on the bottom. This works only in areas where the fishermen know that flounders are schooled in dense masses.

Channel catfish and blue catfish are quite popular with many fresh water fishermen, but these fish are very rarely taken on artificial lures. The fellow who seeks these fish will enjoy much better luck using natural baits.

Following is a list of popular fresh and salt water fish with general types of lures these fish will strike. Although flies and fly fishing are not discussed in this book, flies are listed for the fish that will take them readily. The order of listing—plugs, spoons, jigs, etc.—does not indicate first, second, third, etc., choices, but rather just the types of most productive lures for the fish designated.

FRESH WATER

BLACK BASS—All actions and types of plugs, spoons, jigs, spinners, plastic worms, flies.

SMALLMOUTH BASS—Same type artificials as black bass; less inclined than black bass to hit surface lures.

SPOTTED BASS—Same lures as black bass.

WHITE BASS—Small spoons, jigs, spinner combinations, sinking flies.

YELLOW BASS—Small plugs, spoons, jigs, plastic worms, flies.

ROCK BASS—Small jigs, spinners; rarely plugs, spoons.

MUSKELLUNGE—Large underwater plugs, spoons.

NORTHERN PIKE—Large underwater plugs, spoons, jigs; occasionally surface plugs in shallow, grassy water.

PICKEREL—Medium size underwater plugs, spoons.

WALLEYE—Medium size deep running plugs, spoons, plastic worms.

RAINBOW TROUT—Small underwater plugs, spoons, spinners, flies.

BROOK TROUT—Flies, small underwater plugs, spinners.

LAKE TROUT—Large underwater and deep running plugs, spoons.

BROWN TROUT—Flies, small spoons, spinners.

CUTTHROAT TROUT—Flies, small plugs, spoons, spinners.

DOLLY VARDEN TROUT—Flies, small plugs, spoons, spinners.

GOLDEN TROUT—Flies, small spinners.

ATLANTIC SALMON—Mainly flies; occasionally taken on small plugs, spoons.

KING SALMON—Large underwater plugs, spoons.

LANDLOCKED SALMON—Spoons, spinners.

COHO—Large underwater plugs, spoons.

WHITE CRAPPIE—Very small underwater plugs, spoons, jigs, spinners, plastic worms, flies.

BLACK CRAPPIE—Same lures as white crappie.

BLUEGILL—Very small underwater plugs, jigs, spinners, flies.

WHITE PERCH—Same lures as white crappie.

ARCTIC GRAYLING—Very small underwater plugs, spinners, flies.

CHANNEL CATFISH—Occasionally small plugs, plastic worms fished on bottom; other lure types not recommended.

BLUE CATFISH—Rarely taken on lures of any type.

BULLHEAD—Rarely taken on lures of any type.

CARP—Rarely taken on lures of any type.

SALT WATER

ALBACORE—Rapidly moving shallow running spoons, jigs.

AMBERJACK—Medium to deep running plugs, spoons, jigs.

BARRACUDA—All types of lures; surface plugs in shallow water.

BLACK SEA BASS—Rarely taken on lures of any type.

WHITE SEA BASS—Deep running plugs, spoons, jigs.

GIANT SEA BASS—Rarely taken on lures of any type.

SEA BASS—Small spoons, jigs.

STRIPPED BASS—Underwater plugs, spoons, jigs, spinners; occasionally surface plugs in shallow water.

The gafftopsail catfish is a favorite of many salt water fishermen, but going after them with lures is a waste of time. These fish prefer natural baits.

CHANNEL BASS—Spoons, jigs; small channel bass frequently take deep running plugs, spoons, plastic worms.

BLUEFISH—Medium depth plugs, spoons, jigs.

BONEFISH—Flies; all types very small lures fished slow on bottom

BONITA—Rapidly moving shallow running spoons, jigs.

COBIA—Floating-diving to medium depth plugs, spoons.

DOLPHIN—All types of lures, except strictly surface ones.

BLACK DRUM—Plastic worms; occasionally jigs.

FLOUNDER—Occasionally plastic worms, jigs; rarely take any other types of lures.

KING MACKEREL—Large shallow running plugs, spoons, jigs.

SPANISH MACKEREL—Small shallow running plugs, spoons, jigs.

BLUE MARLIN—Infrequently large feathered jigs; rarely taken on other type lures.

WHITE MARLIN—Same as blue marlin.

POMPANO—Small bottom-bumping plugs, spoons, jigs, plastic worms.

SNOOK—Medium size underwater plugs, spoons; also flies.

TARPON—Large floating-diving to medium depth underwater plugs, spoons; small tarpon readily take flies in brackish waters.

WAHOO—Rapidly moving shallow running spoons, jigs.

SPOTTED SEA TROUT—All types of medium size lures; occasionally surface lures in shallow water or at night.

SEA TROUT—Same lures as spotted sea trout.

PACIFIC YELLOWTAIL—Underwater to deep running plugs, spoons, jigs.

RED SNAPPER—Occasionally very deep running small plugs, jigs, plastic worms.

CROAKER—Occasionally small jigs on bottom; rarely any other types of lures.

WHITING—Occasionally small jigs, spinners on bottom; rarely any other types of lures.

GAFFTOPSAIL CATFISH—Occasionally small plugs fished on bottom; rarely any other types of lures.

SEA CATFISH—Rarely take any types of lures.

SHARKS—Rarely take any types of lures.

25

HOT AND COLD

A wader had just come in from the surf, dragging a stringer of several dozen speckled trout behind him. Sights like this attract onlookers like picnics draw ants, and inevitably someone will ask what bait was used. That question was put to the wader. He wiggled a spoon dangling from the end of his fishing rod and answered: "That gold spoon was hot, real hot today."

I was standing nearby with my youngest daughter, Laura June. She asked me what the fellow meant by saying the spoon was "hot." I explained it was only a slang expression meaning that the fish just had a liking for that particular spoon that day, and that it had nothing to do with the temperature.

"But what happens if that man uses it when the water is real cold?" she asked. Anyone with children knows that ten year olds can be real inquisitive, and at times ask questions that require answers of considerable explanation. So in a way Laura June is responsible for this chapter.

Water temperature—hot, cold or in between—is important in overall fishing. Although lure action, presentation, and manipulation are the prime factors in lure fishing, water temperature does have some bearing. Its bearing, however, is not on lure action or color, but rather on the depths at which the lure should be fished.

The man who goes salt water fishing for such migratory fish like Spanish mackerel, king mackerel, dolphin, etc., will wear out his arm casting if the water is cold. These fish will not be there. These fish prefer waters that range from 75 to 90 degrees. This temperature must be in a zone from surface to about 10 feet deep, and this in turn dictates that shallow running lures are in order.

The same man seeking speckled trout in salt water will find specks go deep when the water temperature goes 80 degrees or above. This, of course, means that deep running lures must be used.

A number of temperature studies have been made on fresh

water fish. The fact that fresh water fish can be held within the confines of a lake means that the movements of these fish can be traced by means of electronic fish-finding devices. Their depths can be accurately located and then the temperature of that area can be determined with a fishing thermometer. The result of all this information has produced some rather exact temperature zones for many species of fish. Consequently the fellow who uses a fishing thermometer and fish-finding electronic gear will score every time. That is, of course, if he knows the preferred temperature zone for the species of fresh water fish he seeks.

Remember that fresh water fish are not migratory. They can't travel north or south to find water of a suitable temperature range. They have to travel up and down. One day water temperature they prefer may be in a strata five feet below the surface, and the next day—or even later on the same day—it might be 20 feet down. Consequently a lure worked at five feet will produce little when the fish are 20 feet down.

Water temperature influences the activities of fish. They are cold-blooded creatures and their bodies take on the temperature of the water in which they swim. Cold winter water slows their metabolism to the point where they eat about one-third to one-fourth less than they do in warm summer water. Take fresh water trout as an example. These fish can not survive in water that runs in excess of 70 degrees. Black bass can not survive in water that consistently stays colder than 50 degrees.

Lakes will stratify into three separate zones during the warm summer months. The warm surface water makes up the top layer which is called the epilimnion. This is the layer that absorbs heat and light from the sun, and it is the layer where plankton blooms. Plankton is what small baitfish feed upon and this is the reason these small fish are found near the surface and the shoreline. The second zone in a lake is called the thermocline, and this middle zone is the one of greatest interest to the fisherman since it provides the water temperature sought by most fish. It is also rich in life-sustaining oxygen. The bottom layer of the lake is where the water is coldest and most dense, and it is called the hypolimnion.

As water cools, it condenses and sinks to the bottom. This holds true until the bottom temperature reaches 39.1 degrees. Then the cold water starts to expand and rise back to the surface. If the temperature keeps dropping, it will eventually freeze and ice will form on the lake.

I mentioned earlier that bass can not survive in water that consistently runs below 50 degrees. Yet bass will survive in lakes on which ice often forms. The reason is that some place between the ice and the bottom they find water tolerable for life.

A temperature range that may be pleasant for one species of fresh water fish can be fatal for another. Black bass can live in most lakes in the United States but not in the lakes of northern Canada. Canadian lakes are fit habitat for lake trout, northern pike, walleyes, and Arctic grayling, but they have a temperature range totally unsuitable for any members of the bass or sunfish family.

Opportune temperature zones for some of the more popular fresh water species are listed in the table below.

Opportune temperature zone	Fish species
68–75	Black bass
65–70	Smallmouth bass
70–75	White bass
68–80	Crappie
68–80	Bluegill
68–75	Channel catfish
60–70	Muskellunge
50–70	Northern pike
55–70	Walleye
65–60	White perch
55–70	Yellow perch
55–75	Brook trout
55–70	Brown trout
45–55	Lake trout
60–70	Rainbow trout

It holds that the deeper the lake, the wider the range of temperatures from surface to bottom. With a fishing thermometer the fisherman can find the opportune zone and present lures accordingly. He can find these same zones without the thermometer, but it will take a lot of experimenting with lures at various depths. And this can indeed be time consuming.

The table listing the opportune temperature zones should not be interpreted to mean that these fish will not be found outside of these ranges.

Quite frequently the ideal temperature zone will not be found in a lake. This is especially true in many of the shallow lakes in the southern United States and Mexico. Still these lakes will produce some fine action for the lure fisheman.

I love to visit the Wildlife Kingdom Fishing Resort near Newton, Texas. It is a resort with eight manmade lakes and cabins with all the comforts of home, except no telephones. The lakes are small. They range from three to 40 acres with maximum depths from 15 to 40 feet. My favorite lake there is about 30 feet at its deepest spot. I have fished this lake and caught a great many black bass in the heat of summer when the water ranged from 90 degrees on the surface to 77 degrees in its deepest hole. The point I am making here is that although fish seek out an opportune zone in which to live, they are just like people in that they will make the best of it even if the Utopia zone is absent.

There are even times when fish will vacate the opportune temperature zone even though it may exist. This is usually when a lake level is changing or when there is a steady, strong wind.

In the lake rising situation, the fish move with the rise to newly flooded flats which will abound with all sorts of fodder. On a rapidly falling lake, these same fish are likely to vacate the thermocline and move into the deep holes. In this case the decreasing water pressure apparently tips off the fish of the impending disaster of being stranded high and dry.

Under strong wind conditions the middle of the lake is not the place to fish, even if you have a seaworthy boat. Work both the windward and lee shorelines, even though the water depth at these points may not be in the opportune temperature zone. The lee shoreline will be good because of the wind blowing insects and bits of food from the shore out into the water. Enough of these tidbits in the water can cause fish to rise above the opportune temperature zone. Over on the windward shoreline the wind will buffet schools of small baitfish into shallow water, and again the gamefish are likely to rise up and follow in for easy feedings.

26

ON LURES ONLY

SPORTS and vacation shows are held annually in many of America's major cities, and there is large representation from the lure industry at each of these shows. The question most frequently asked by visitors to the various booths is: "Will this lure really catch fish?" Obviously the lure representative—even if it is a publicity doll in a bikini—will answer in the affirmative.

The question can be answered more impressively by letting me relate some personal experiences in fishing artificial lures.

In June of 1968 Larry Ferrill of Aledo, Texas, and Christie Hance of Lafayette, La., partners in the operation of Altex Outdoor Clubs, hosted 10 Texas and Louisiana outdoor writers on a fishing trip to Saskatchewan Province and the Northwest Territories in Canada.

Although the party on the airplane included 14, only 12 participated in the fishing. In four days of fishing—two out of Camp Grayling on Black Lake in Saskatchewan and two on lakes Lady Grey, Tsu and King in the Northwest Territories—we caught and released approximately 550 lake trout, northern pike, walleyes and Arctic grayling. Actually the 550 figure is a little low for some of the fellows told me they did not count a number of two and three pound northern pike caught. But whether it was 550 or 580 fish, each and every one was caught on an artificial lure.

We started our fishing at Black Lake using lures the Chipwyean Indian guides recommended. Invariably these were big spoons. Some of our party stuck with spoons during the entire week long trip. Others, including the writer, experimented after the first day. We found that even though spoons were preferred by the fish, particularly the northern pike and lake trout, they also went for plugs, jigs and even plastic worms often enough to keep the action from becoming dull.

Most of the northern pike ranged seven to 10 pounds in size,

Lake trout show a preference for large deep running lures. *Houston (Texas) Post* Outdoor Editor, Harv Boughton, caught this 37-pounder trolling in Black Lake in Saskatchewan Province in Canada.

Small lake trout often move into shallow water. Trans Texas Airways pilot Bob Street uses pliers to hold up this laker because of fish's sharp teeth. The sharp teeth dictate using a short wire leader.

Another fish that shows a decided preference for artificial lures is the
northern pike. Chipwyean Indian guide Boniface Buck exhibits pike
author caught casting on lake in Saskatchewan Province, Canada.

with me having the luck of getting the biggest, a 16 pounder. Most of our lake trout ran six to eight pounds. The biggest was a 37-pounder trolled out of Black Lake by Houston, Texas, *Post* Outdoor Editor Harv Boughton. Roy Swann of the Corpus Christi, Texas, *Caller-Times* caught a 25 pound laker casting from the rocky shoreline on King Lake. Other big ones included 18 and 14 pounders by Ed Holder, Port Arthur, Texas, *News* Outdoor Editor.

Again let me repeat that all these fish were caught on artificial lures. Even though none in our group fished with live or natural bait, I had the opportunity to talk with three fishermen who did. One was from another resort lodge near Camp Grayling. I ran across him when I was walking the shoreline the third day at Black Lake. He was thrilled with the Canadian fishing and told me that the previous day he had caught 22 northern pike in just two hours. He kept his limit and had released the rest. All were taken on live bait, but his biggest fish barely made four pounds. The point I am making here is that he caught more fish in a short time on live bait, but we caught bigger fish on artificial lures. Lures gave us the "quality" discussed in an earlier chapter.

Now to the other two bait fishermen. I ran across them in the hotel bar in Fort Smith, N.W.T. They reported catching a large number of lake trout in a short period of time, but none of their fish went over five pounds. Our writers group using lures exclusively caught very few fish less than five pounds.

There seems to be a message there that if one is going for trophy fish, go armed with artificial lures. This message can be further substantiated by noting how many winners in *Field & Stream* Magazine's annual fishing contests make their catches on lures.

Every winter at Galveston, Texas, Offat's Bayou, a nearly landlocked body of salt water, pays off with excellent hauls of speckled trout. The bayou is quite deep and in sudden cold spells the specks move into the deep holes in big schools. This usually comes at a time when live bait is unobtainable at any price. Consequently a fellow has a choice of using lures or staying at home. When these trout runs are in full swing, it is common to see several hundred boats with two to three fishermen each on this bayou that measures two miles long by a half mile at its widest part. And all these fishermen will be pitching lures—and catching fish. At times like this even the live bait dealers begrudgingly stock up on artificial lures.

Up on Lake Ouachita in Arkansas, there used to be a guide who placed lures, particularly plugs, on a pedestal with the Bible. If you showed up at the boat landing with a bait bucket, he would refuse to take you out, even if it meant giving up a paying trip for the day. Not only that he would take fiendish delight in moving into an area where folks were catching black bass on live bait—and then proceed to show them up using artificial lures. The odd part of it all was that he really had no preference in the make or brand of a plug. What little preference he showed was in regards to finishes and colors. He regarded a shad finish as best. After that he preferred plugs with red, yellow, white, black or combinations of these colors. I imagine the only reason he never tied in with a plug manufacturer to promote a certain line was because he was so extremely difficult to get along with. He was a cussed old cuss from the word "go."

I know a number of guides who have ties with lure companies but I have only met one who tried to force customers to use the

Proof that fish hit lures. This is part of a one-day catch of lake trout made by Texas outdoor writers on Altex Outdoor Clubs trip to Canadian Northwest Territories. Group using artificial lures only caught limits of lake trout, northern pike and walleyes daily for five days straight.

lures he promoted. The· others would give sales pitches for the brands they were pushing, but if you desired to use rival makes, they let it go at that—and still gave you your money's worth in fish-finding and guide service.

This brings up another interesting point about lures. I have the advantage of fishing with a number of different lure manufacturers or their factory representatives. Just about every time this happens, they will give me a half dozen or so of the lures they market—and then they will go through my tackle box to borrow and use lures made by rival companies. The first time this happened was back when as an outdoors writer I was still wet behind the ears. I actually suspected that my fishing partner, a successful Southwest lure manufacturer, did not have faith in his own products.

The expression on my face must have telegraphed him my thoughts. With a big smile on his face he remarked: "You know, some of the best ideas for new lures come from rival products."

I am sure that major automobile manufacturers thoroughly test models of rival companies. They may not admit it, but under cover of darkness or on some barren wilderness road, someone in the organization will shakedown rival cars for ideas about what and what not to do on their own future models.

It is a form of "brain picking."

27

ON TACKLE BOXES

THE biggest mistake the lure fisherman can make is to go out and purchase the wrong size tackle box. The box that looks the right size in the tackle store will be too small when the fellow gets it home. When it comes to size for a tackle box, my advice is to select the one you feel is big enough, and then purchase one just a little bit bigger. If you are a serious lure fisherman, even that box in time will get too small. As far as I am concerned, there is no such thing as a too big tackle box.

The mistake fishermen make is to purchase a tackle box with just lures in mind. When you get down to the actual mechanics of fishing, this just does not work because there are a few other items you must take along if you expect to have an enjoyable fishing trip.

There are eight tackle boxes in my family—and I still don't have room to pack in everything. And then if I could get everything into a single box, it would be too heavy to pick up. Just let me list what is packed in one of my fresh water tackle boxes. It contains 44 lures, two spools of extra line, a spare reel, fish stringer, pliers, nail clippers, fish knife, three assortments of hooks, four assortments of sinkers, two plastic containers of terminal hardware (swivels, snaps, line connectors, etc.), leader material, screwdriver, insect repellent, reel lubricant, ferrule cement, plastic tape, four bottles of model airplane lacquer, snake bite kit, an assortment of floats and a spare length of nylon rope.

Some of the items may never be used, but I still want them there. For example, I hope I never have to use the snake bite kit, but when I think of some of the places I go to fish, the presence of the kit in the tackle box is comforting. That spare length of nylon rope came in handy once in helping to tie up the boat to ride out a sudden squall.

One of the author's many tackle boxes. This one made of wood can be used as extra seat when lid is closed. Disadvantage of wood box is that it soaks up moisture and requires a lot of upkeep.

Modern tackle boxes marketed today come in wood, plastic, steel and aluminum. I have at least one of each material, and each has its advantages and disadvantages. Wood is strong and when the box is closed it will serve as an extra seat. Unfortunately the wood absorbs moisture and presents a constant cleaning problem. Steel is even stronger than wood, but it is heavy and it will rust—more cleaning and upkeep problems. Aluminum is light and strong, but it is noisy. Plastic is light and quiet, but it can become brittle and break. And there always seems to be someone around to accidentally step or sit on these boxes. So when purchasing a box, a fellow must consider what abuse it may face.

Boxes come with all sorts of tray and compartment arrangements. The salt water fisherman will want a box with large compartments since most of his lures will be large. The spin fisherman will need a box with smaller compartments. I have a friend whose wife decided to give him a new tackle box for Christmas. Not being interested in fishing herself, she did not know what her husband needed. She plunked down $24.95 in a tackle store and surprised her husband with a six-trayed box with individual compartments for 70 lures. Her husband was indeed surprised because he was a salt water fisherman and his lures were too big to fit into the compartments.

Size is not the only thing that must be taken into consideration when purchasing a tackle box. Pay particular attention to the latches, fittings and hinges. They should be rust-proof and well made, for these are usually the first points to give you trouble. A lock on a box discourages theft and borrowing. I like a lock for one other reason. Every time I close my box—even when fishing—I lock it. Just knock an open tackle box off a boat seat and you, too, will learn to keep the box locked.

A tackle box, regardless how much it cost, is only as good as the care you give it. Periodically empty the box and thoroughly clean it. Put a drop or two of oil on all metal working parts. Any metal parts showing signs of rust should be sanded clean and then painted over. After every fishing trip leave the box open for a day so that it will thoroughly air out and dry.

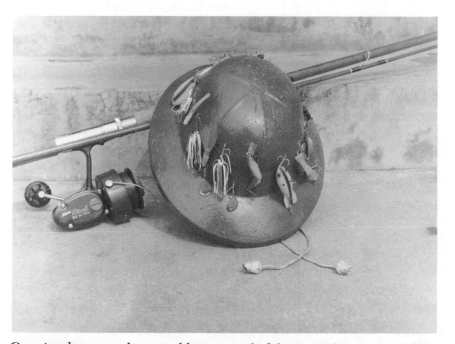

Carrying lures can be a problem in wade-fishing. Author has styrofoam sun helmet expressly for this kind of fishing. Several dozen lures can be carried safely in this manner by imbedding the hooks in the helmet.

There will be times when the lure fisherman will be unable to pack along his big tackle box. It is impossible to wade fish and lug along a big box. Still the fisherman will need some means of carrying along extra lures. The plastic boxes that lures come in are fine for this purpose. You can stuff about a half dozen of these boxes in your pockets. Or the fisherman can purchase a small compartmented box with hinged lid. Such a box is small enough to stuff in a hip pocket, yet it has sufficient room for about five or six lures.

Personally I prefer to use the "fishing hat" when I go wade-fishing. I have two. One is a styrafoam sun helmet and the other is a straw hat. I carry lures on the helmet by imbedding the hooks in the soft plastic. On the straw hat the lure hooks are stuck under the straw weavings. When I want to change lures, it is a simple matter of taking off the hat and taking off the lure I desire to use. It beats carrying lures in plastic boxes in my pockets for I often wade out in water chest deep.

28

WHY SO MANY BRANDS

LURE brand popularity varies tremendously from area to area. Plug A that may be a number one seller in one part of the state may run a poor 25th in another part of the same state even though the waters fished and fish sought are basically the same in both areas. This difference in popularity is not a matter of the fish being discriminating. Instead it is a case of the preferences of the regular lure fishermen in any given area.

Retail tackle shops stock the types and brand name lures that they have the most calls for. They will not stock new types unless they can visualize sales for them.

For every brand name that has national distribution, there are scores more that enjoy only sectional or state distribution. Many of these smaller companies have been in operation for a number of years, but they don't have national distribution because of the expense involved. This expense is a major one of sales personnel and sales personnel travel. It is no easy job to get a new lure introduced into a territory. Wholesalers who handle these territories are tough customers to sell. They are extremely price conscious, and they will not stock up on items unless they feel the items will sell reasonably fast.

For example, if a wholesale distributor is faced with making a decision on two spoons that appear to be almost identical, he will invariably go for the one with the lower price tag for he knows that the majority of the fishermen using lures are rather price conscious. The suggested retail price of a lure has a lot to do with the movement of that lure. A too high or a too low retail price can hurt a lure. If the price is ridiculously low, many fishermen will shun the lure because they figure there must be something wrong with it to sell that cheap. This is probably the main reason many Japanese copies of successful American lures don't sell well.

A high retail price can be just as bad. Let me use as example what happened with a name brand spoon on the upper Texas coast in 1968. I will refer to it as Spoon A. Twice in the space of a year the manufacturer raised the price of the spoon. Meanwhile a lesser known manufacturer came out with what I will refer to as Spoon B. The two spoons were almost identical in size, shape and weight. The suggested retail price for Spoon B was 25 cents beneath that of the nationally known Spoon A.

One wholesale distributor who had pushed Spoon A for years cut his orders by 75 per cent. What he cut from Spoon A company, he spent with Spoon B company. In selling to his retail outlets, the retailers followed suit in their purchases, and at the time of this writing Spoon B, which has proven to be a good fish-getter, is moving very well. I asked the distributor if he planned to drop the Spoon A line completely.

"No, I can't afford to do that," he explained. "I'll keep just a minimum on hand because my retailers will always have some customers who will accept no substitutes."

He went on to explain that shelf display in the retail tackle store has a lot to do with establishing a lure in an area. If a manufacturer can't get his line displayed prominently on retail shelves, his line stands little chance of becoming popular.

On an extended fishing trip in the Florida Keys some years back, I had an interesting experience with the popularity of lures. I happened to take along a number of lures that I had used successfully in salt water fishing on the Texas coast. In visiting a number of tackle shops in the Keys, I didn't see a single display of any of the brands I had. The reason was that my lures were made by small Texas companies that did not have wide distribution.

I used my own lures and caught a heck of a lot of fish. The word got around the motel that there was a Texas outdoor writer cleaning up on fish. Naturally I had a lot of the motel guests knock on my door to find out what I was using. I showed them the lures and thought no more about it until I dropped into a nearby tackle shop to buy some leader material. The word of my catches had also gotten to the owner. He good naturedly kidded me about my catches causing him problems. He explained that he had several dozen visitors drop into his store wanting to buy some of the brand lures I was using.

"I sold some of them plugs almost like yours," he said, "but I guess about half of them said they would try another tackle store. You know, I doubt if there is a tackle store in Florida with any plugs of the brand you're carrying. This sort of thing happens every now and then when someone comes down here and uses his plugs and spoons from home."

It's obvious that if a tackle shop attempted to keep in stock every lure brand made or asked for, the owner would have a prohibitively high inventory that would eventually drive him out of business.

The bulk of the lures stocked in the average tackle shop will be those that the natives of the area use most frequently. After all, the natives are his bread and butter customers, and it is their repeat business that keeps the shop owner in business. This is the reason that in visiting tackle stores from one section to another, one will find different brand names predominating.

This does not mean that tackle stores won't try to push new brands. They will if they can get a good buy at the right price. Getting these new brands established is then a matter of getting out samples and good shelf display.

The first step is to get a list of regular fishermen well known within the area and pass out samples to them. All these fishermen have to do is catch fish on the lures and talk about their catches. Plenty of listeners will trek to the store to buy "some of those plugs Joe caught his fish on." The second step is for the store to prominently and attractively display the lure brands it is seeking to push.

One store owner described it to me this way:

"A lot of fishermen come in here to buy lures. They hear the fish were hitting well on red and white plugs, and that is what they want. Usually they don't remember brand names, so they will start picking out red and white plugs that catch their attention quickest. I display the line I'm pushing in front of everything else. Most lure fishermen go for the brand that has the most lures displayed. For instance, if I wanted to sell out my stock of Brand A spoons, I would put them all on display together. Fishermen just seem to feel that if a display has a 100 Brand A spoons in it and the rack next to it has only a dozen Brand B spoons, then the big display must be of the lures the fish like. Now when that rack of 100 spoons gets down to a dozen or so, then sales for that brand fall off and fishermen start going to whatever other brand is well represented. When it comes to buying lures, fishermen are a lot like women in buying on impulse."

Generally speaking lures that have national distribution retail for 15 to 30 cents more than lures that have only sectional distribution.

29

GLOSSARY

BAIL—A part of spinning reel which picks up line on retrieve.

BAIT-CASTING REEL—Multiplying reel with free-spooling device and level wind.

BAIT-CASTING ROD—Light rod with stiff backbone and whippy tip to cast plugs and spoons.

BARB—A projecting spike that points backward on the point of a hook.

BEND—Curve of fish hook.

BITE—The space between the bend and shank of a fish hook; also taking of bait or lure into fish's mouth.

BOBBER—Cork or plastic float which keeps bait or lure off the bottom; also to signal bite of fish when it goes beneath water's surface.

BUCKTAIL—Hair from deer's tail tied around small metal eye and used as extra action device on lures.

CHUGGER—Term for plug that has type of face that causes "chug" sound in water.

EYE—Part of hook to which leader is tied.

FLOAT—A cork or plastic bobber.

FLOATER—Term applied to lure that floats and remains on surface during entire retrieve.

FLY—Artificial lure of fur, silk and feathers tied on a very small hook.

FLY-FISHING—A specialized type of fishing in which flies are used.

HARDWARE—Slang term for artificial lures.

LEADER—Nylon or gut material used between line and hook or lure.

LINE CONNECTOR—Elongated metal device used to connect line to leader or leader to lure.

LIP—Metal or plastic flange at front of plug to cause it to dive, wiggle or disturb surface of water on retrieve.

LURE—Any artificial bait.

PLUG—Plastic or wooden lure fitted with hooks.

PLUGGING—Term applied to fishing with plugs.

POPPING FLOAT—Float that has concaved face to make distinct "pop" sound in water when rod is jerked sharply.

POPPING BUG—Small cork or plastic plug with concaved face that makes sharp "pop" sound in water when rod is twitched.

RAY—A spine supporting fish's fin.

SCREW-EYE—Eyed screw for purpose of attaching hooks to lure.

SET THE HOOK—Forcing the hook past the barb into the flesh in fish's mouth.

SHANK—Part of hook between the eye and the bend.

SKIRT—Shredded rubber or plastic dressing that flutters on retrieve.

SPIN-CAST REEL—Closed face reel with oscillating spool and trigger device to free line for casting.

SPIN-CAST ROD—Light rod specially designed for spin-cast fishing.

SPINNER—Metal lure that spins on an axis when retrieved.

SPINNING REEL—Reel with fixed spool and bail which picks up line when handle is turned.

SPINNING ROD—Light rod with large guides.

SPLIT RING—Twin ring with splits to permit attaching hooks to lures.

SPOON—A metal lure, usually flat or slightly curved.

STRIKE—Grab of fish at lure or bait.

SPREADER—Item of terminal tackle designed to keep two or more hooks or lures apart without tangling.

TEASER—A hookless device used in conjunction with a lure or bait to attract fish to the lure or bait.

TERMINAL TACKLE—Items attached to end of line; includes leader, snaps, swivels, hooks, lures, etc.

TIP TOP—Final guide on rod tip through which the line runs.

TROLL—Towing or dragging a lure or bait behind a moving boat.

Index